WOMEN

of AUSTRALIA

WOMEN
of AUSTRALIA

THEIR LIVES AND TIMES: A PHOTOGRAPHIC GALLERY

Selected and with commentary by Ingrid Ohlsson and Helen Duffy

MACMILLAN
Pan Macmillan Australia

First published 1999 in Macmillan by Pan Macmillan Australia Pty Limited

St Martins Tower, 31 Market Street, Sydney

Produced by Ross, Hutchinson & Associates, 52 Cambridge St, Collingwood, Victoria 3066, Australia

Production editor: Peter Ascot

Designed by Phil Campbell

National Library of Australia

Cataloguing-in-Publication data:

Ohlsson, Ingrid.

Women of Australia: their life and times, a photographic gallery.

ISBN 0 7329 0987 2.

1. Women – Australia – Social conditions – Pictorial works.

2. Women – Australia – History – Pictorial works. I. Duffy, Helen. II. Title.

305.40994

Printed in Singapore

CONTENTS

INTRODUCTION

This collection of photographs, spanning one-and-a-half centuries, offers a visual chronicle of the lives and times of Australian women. Due to the elementary nature of 19th-century photography, the selection is eclectic, relying on surviving images that have been preserved in archival institutions and family albums. The 20th-century photographs are more wide-ranging, with significant contributions by some of our best photojournalists and professional photographers. There are famous and well-known pictures, included here for their outstanding contribution to any historical perspective, while others have not been published before, sourced from a range of people and places and included for the insight they provide on everyday life and times. It is obviously impossible to include all women who deserve attention in these pages. Our famous women, remarkable for their achievements in the arts, sport and public and professional life, are well represented, but it is the lives of ordinary women, revealed through a series of evocative images, which tell the real story of what it is to have been born female in Australia.

Unfortunately there is very little photographic record of the convict era. The first 'photograph', the daguerreotype, was produced in 1837 and provided a single image only on a metal plate. It was soon superseded by Englishman William Talbot's invention of the negative-positive process, whereby multiple prints could be made for the first time. The first commercial photographer in Australia was George Goodman, who set up a studio in Sydney in 1842. He concentrated on portraiture, as did the handful of other photographers who established studios in other capital cities. Their images are generally contrived portraits, sometimes in situ (such as J. W. Lindt's stylised studio portraits of Aborigines taken in the 1870s).

It was the invention of the plate glass negative in 1851 that really made photography a popular profession. By the late 1850s the middle classes had embraced the *carte-de-visite*, a visiting card depicting a small family portrait. Photographic studios became more numerous. Considering the fragility of glass plate negatives and the cumbersome nature of transportation, it is remarkable that so many photographs of outback life survive. Baldwin Spencer's wonderful photographs of Aborigines in central Australia were taken under the most extreme conditions, using a black tent as a mobile dark room.

The invention that made photography possible for the majority of households by the end of the 1880s was George Eastman's invention of roll film, closely followed by his Kodak box brownie camera, which went on sale for five shillings. The box brownie, and the increasing number of itinerant photographers who took it upon themselves to chronicle rural and city life, have left an extraordinarily vivid pictorial history of the late 19th and early 20th centuries. And the subjects are women more often than not. Outback pioneers in their Sunday best are juxtaposed with their harsh surroundings – lined up with their children in front of crudely built slab huts. Such photographs are all the more poignant for the hardships not pictured but clearly present in the isolation of the bush environment. In contrast are the lives of the well-to-do, often captured taking tea on manicured lawns or indulging in a genteel game of croquet.

While the demands of advertising and news saw photography turn into an industry in the 1920s and 1930s, certain talented individuals took it to the level of an artform. Photographers such as Sam Hood, Olive Cotton, Max Dupain, Pat Holmes and David Moore may have been sent to cover the local baby competition or an advertising gig, but they returned with images that managed to alert us to the beauty, interest, humour and liveliness of everyday existence. The massive newsworthiness of World War II gave press photographers pre-eminence (included here are some memorable wartime images by Damien Parer), and ever since we have looked to them for our daily supply of pictures. It has been their job to capture the first-born baby on New Year's Day, the child's first day at school, the professional achievers, the heart-wrenching images of fire, flood and drought. Numerous photographs are reproduced from the pages of the nation's newspapers, the work of some of Australia's most highly respected photojournalists, such as Bruce Postle and John Lamb. Today, photography is in the hands of anyone who can hold a camera, such is the nature of the technology, but we still look to the specialists to point out what is rich or hidden or unusual in our visual field – photographers such as portraitist Jacqueline Mitelman, and the chronicler of the arts, life and everything else, Ponch Hawkes.

Divided into ten broad themes, this collection tells the story of marriage and motherhood, childhood and schooldays, domesticity and leisure, professional occupations and pleasures, failures and achievements. And inherent in the pictorial story is the evolving role of women in our society; the struggle for equality, for equal rights and equal pay. In the dramatic images taken during periods of great social upheaval, in war and depression, we witness not only the tremendous changes that have occurred in women's lives but also the immutable experiences common to women of all generations.

Ingrid Ohlsson & Helen Duffy

MOTHERS AND DAUGHTERS

Birth, childhood and the getting of wisdom

A British visitor in 1880 complained of the 'supremacy' of babies in the colony. He noted how the presence of children dominated the household, and how their mothers carted them here and there around the land. The British practice of tucking children away in the nursery or in a pram down the garden never really took off in Australia. This was partly due to the lack of servants, but more so to the informal nature of Australian society.

Women's lives have been inextricably linked to and determined by the lives of their children. In 19th-century Australia, when women were producing on average six or seven children, the biggest risk to their health was childbirth, but the greatest threat to their peace of mind was the health of their children. Motherhood was a state 'never over, never forgotten'.

Children born female had barely left their mother's side before they themselves became mothers and were plunged into the intimate and seemingly endless cycle of maternity. Childhood, for many in the 19th century, hardly existed or was all too brief a stage. But circumstances improved. Primary school education became standard for six to 13 year olds in the 1860s, and state secondary education was introduced in the 1880s. Attending school gave girls respite from the toil of domestic duties, and the chance to socialise, exercise and learn the lessons that might just provide an alternative in the future.

In the 20th century, the gap between childhood and motherhood widened over the generations, and girls of all classes found themselves with previously unthought of opportunities. According to a recent survey, teenage girls of today predict that they will be in satisfying careers and be bearing satisfying children by age 35. Judging by the ferocious will of their female forebears, these seem to be not unreasonable expectations.

FACING PAGE: Despite the fact that Australia is one of the most urbanised countries in the world, it is still life on the land that stirs the national imagination. And when it comes to images of girlhood, it is the nuggety youngsters of the bush who seem to have the strongest hold on our heartstrings. Kerry Buckleigh, of Beaconsfield, Victoria, is pictured here during a trip to Melbourne for the Royal Agricultural Show.

ABOVE: For many women in 19th-century Australia, childbirth was a dangerous undertaking. More women died delivering their children than from any other cause. Women in remote areas often had no access to medical help, while those who did would have sometimes been better off without it: childbed fever, the biggest danger for postnatal mothers, was found to be caused by doctors delivering babies without following simple hygiene procedures. Women, of course, had no choice but to try to ignore the statistics. This photograph of a composed and prosperous Mrs Cooper is unusual, as pregnant women were not generally subjects for the camera.

ABOVE: The birthrate in Australia has been on a steady decline since the late 19th century. A Royal Commission set up in 1904 to examine the falling rate concluded among other things that women's 'unwillingness to submit to the strain and worry of children' and their 'love of luxury' contributed to the problem. Those who continued to have large families in the 20th century, such as this immigrant Dutch family pictured at Melbourne's Royal Women's Hospital, were aided by special welfare endowments that were introduced to ensure that women kept producing children in the numbers necessary to fill the empty continent.

RIGHT: Access to maternal and child health care was one of the earliest women's 'issues' in Australia. Public health authorities resisted the idea of lying-in wards for birthing women. On the goldfields obstetrics were actually banned from the hospitals as the health needs of miners were considered more important. Women responded by setting up their own hospitals, as was the case with the Royal Women's Hospital in Melbourne in 1856. By the mid-20th century, birth had evolved into a highly medicalised procedure. Here, a domiciliary nurse at the Royal Women's Hospital dons a mask to examine a newborn.

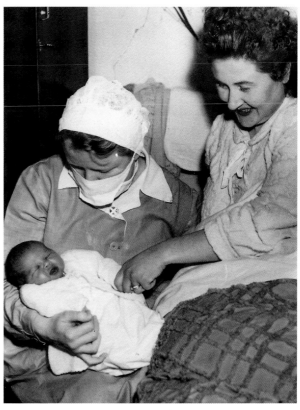

ABOVE: The most extensive and sustained example of a society acting against the interests of its children was the systemised removal of Aboriginal children from their families, a practice that began informally in the 19th century and continued on into the 1960s. Many of the children were placed in institutions, such as these three girls from the Retta Dixon Home in Darwin, pictured in the early 1960s. Others were adopted into white households. The extent of the dispossession that these children and their families suffered was exposed in the 1997 'Stolen Children' Royal Commission.

LEFT: A young Aboriginal woman and child, probably from the Wallaga Lake mission on the southern New South Wales coast, photographed in 1905 by William Henry Corkhill.

ABOVE: Traditional birth practices of Aboriginal women had more in common with those found in birthing centres of modern hospitals than with European methods of the 19th century. Women were encouraged to take up 'active' birth positions; they held their babies immediately; the umbilical cord was left uncut for some time; and activity was encouraged immediately after the birth. Breastfeeding remained the sensible option for Aboriginal women – and poor white women – from the 1920s to the 1960s, a period when many of their middle-class counterparts were swapping breast for bottle, often on medical advice. Well-known photographer Axel Poignant captured this Aboriginal woman nursing her newborn baby in 1942.

ABOVE: Despite the inherently fraught nature of childbirth and early childhood in 19th-century Australia, women derived enormous pleasure and purpose from their offspring – particularly when the children were cleaned and dressed, and under control for the purpose of having their photo taken. This early-1900s family portrait is of Mrs McNamara, of Burraga, New South Wales, and her two well-starched children.

FACING PAGE: Photographer W.H. Corkhill chronicled life at the end of the 19th century in and around the small rural town of Central Tilba, on the New South Wales south coast. The subject to which he turned repeatedly was family life, producing some of Australia's most informal impressions of Victorian and Edwardian households. Pictured here is the photographer's wife, Frances, with their three children, c.1898.

FACING PAGE: For women carrying the full burden of home and family responsibilities, the help of sympathetic female family members in times of childbirth and illness was an invaluable resource. But large extended families would have been scarce in a country that was barely settled and with shorter life expectancy than today, which makes this photograph (c.1905) of four generations of women from New South Wales a rarity.

ABOVE: In this 1895 photograph by anthropologist Baldwin Spencer, two Aranda women of the Alice Springs district watch over a beautifully plump baby. The child lies in a *pitchi*, a carved cradle of wood that was used until the child was old enough to sit astride its mother's hip. Spencer regularly travelled to central and northern Australia between 1894 and 1927 to record the then little understood culture of Aboriginal tribes.

ABOVE: The 'professionalisation' of motherhood was accompanied by a rise in maternal competitiveness. Women who slaved away making healthy children in the isolation of their homes looked forward to the chance to frock up their progeny and show off the results of their labours. Sam Hood, of Sydney, photographed these bonnetted babes and their hatted mothers at the Campsie Baby Show in 1934 for the *Labor Daily* newspaper.

RIGHT: With the establishment of the infant welfare movement in the 1920s, motherhood turned into something of a science. What had been an intimate affair centred mostly on the home became the domain of experts, professionals and politicians. Knowledge of infant health and nutrition expanded enormously, and busy mothers did their best to incorporate a raft of new childcare procedures into already frantic schedules. Their efforts were rewarded with a plunging infant mortality rate. By the end of the 1930s the rate per 1000 births had dropped from 75 in the early 1900s to 35. Pictured here in Sydney in 1940 is Mrs Kavanagh, recently arrived from Dublin, with her healthy baby daughter Geraldine.

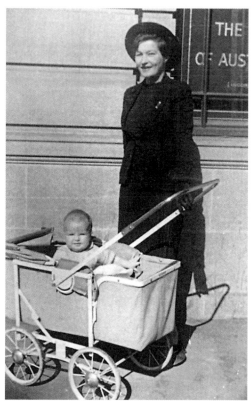

ABOVE: Three generations of women joined together to celebrate a family wedding in Balmain, Sydney, in 1940; the men, some away at the war and others fraternising over a beer, are notably absent from the photograph.

RIGHT: Selina Hassan, pictured here with her three young children in Darwin around 1928, was the granddaughter of one of the thousands of Chinese men who came to Australia to seek their fortune on the goldfields in the 1850s, giving her an Australian lineage longer than most. When Selina's businessman husband died in 1929 she became the provider for her young family, setting up a tailoring and drapery business. In 1940 she took her children to Singapore to ensure they received proper instruction in Chinese religion, and lived under Japanese occupation before returning to Australia to run a newsagency.

ABOVE: The fate that awaited children born in Australia in the
19th and early 20th centuries was an uncertain one. The loss of a
child was by no means the rare event that it is now. In remote
areas, extreme material deprivation and isolation from basic
services were the circumstances that a mother could face as she
delivered yet another child into the raw, hard world of the
Australian outback. This picture of a pioneering mother and her
small family, c.1900, was taken in south-west Western Australia.

ABOVE: Australia was a land of pioneers and battlers, but it was also a place where many a man could generate a fortune and thus provide his family with whatever it was their hearts desired. A.W. Allen was a Sydney solicitor whose regard for his family is not only evident in the spread of presents that greeted his little girls on Christmas Day, 1899, but also in the 51-album photographic chronicle of family life that he compiled from 1890 to 1934.

By the late 1930s, most Australian children were assured of a quality of life for which Australia was to become famous. They had access to education, improving health services and all the distractions that a warm climate and beautiful natural environment could offer. The joy of an Australian childhood is evident in Olive Cotton's image (**ABOVE**) from 1938, while Max Dupain's photograph (**FACING PAGE**) captures something of the experience of growing up in the outback in the 1960s.

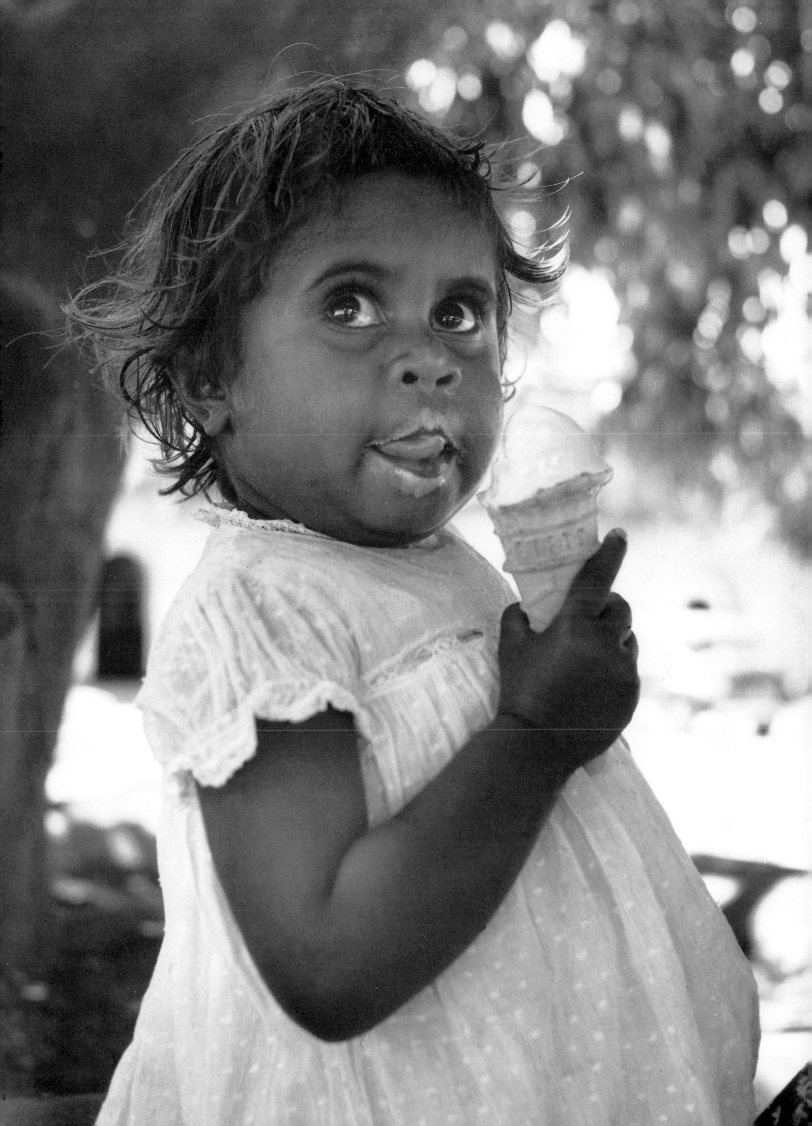

ABOVE: Universal education was introduced to Australia in the 1860s when, according to the historian Manning Clark: 'All boys and girls between the ages of 6 and 13 were about to learn how to read, write, add, subtract, multiply and divide'. This meant, during the primary years at least, that the quality of education received was more likely to depend on wealth and class than gender, and that young girls would be assured of a grounding in the basics at the very least. Pictured here are children playing in the dusty yard of an outback school at Port Hedland in Western Australia in about 1900.

FACING PAGE: At Hobart's Central School in 1914 a group of young students are instructed in a 'physical jerks' regime before class. A more holistic approach to education was beginning to creep into the curriculum of public schools during this period. A program of exercise, dental checks and a variety of other measures would, it was hoped, produce 'superior children'.

ABOVE: There were 72 girls in this primary school class at Erskineville, Sydney, in 1947. Class sizes generally were much larger in those days, but even by accepted standards of the times this class is chronically overcrowded. The problem was due to a serious shortage of teachers that resulted from a parliamentary act allowing for the dismissal of female teachers once they married. No doubt expediency rather than a sense of fairness prompted the repeal of the act in the same year as this photo was taken.

FACING PAGE: Dr Maria Montessori set up her first school in Rome in 1907 and within a few years her remarkable teaching methods had reached Australia's shores. The system, which was aimed at the early years of education, advocated personal growth, creativity and individual responsibility, and maintained that children were to be respected as individuals. Inherent in such a philosophy were notions of equality, which translated into some healthy benefits for young female students. One such person is seen here in 1914 asserting her individuality at the blackboard of the Blackfriars Montessori School in Sydney. There are still schools today that concentrate on the method, while many more have incorporated aspects of its philosophy.

ABOVE: By the 1980s, when these Melbourne quads had their first day of school, class sizes were down, interesting and age-relevant curriculums were in place and generally things were looking good for the Australian child at school.

ABOVE: Despite the constraints of modesty, Australian girls were encouraged towards physical activity. The growing national obsession with the sun and sea necessitated the need for aquatic education. Charles Kerry photographed these girls at a lifesaving class in 1900.

ABOVE: Eurythmics was a form of movement that allowed for some gentle exercise without the participants becoming overheated or inelegant. Perfecting the movements are these girls from St Catherine's School in Waverley, Sydney, in 1944. The Grecian costumes and bare feet contributed to the overall aim of a graceful aesthetic. The exercises were done to music, although all that was required of the girls was that they be 'in time' rather than especially musical.

ABOVE: Prejudice against women's education lingered longest in the tertiary sector; women were admitted to some courses at Sydney and Melbourne universities in the 1870s, but they battled thereafter for places. In contrast, secondary education was opened for all from the 1880s, and the many advocates of female education ensured that the best schools were girls' schools. Sydney Girls High, a state school, was established on a single floor of a city building in 1883, and moved to its present Moore Park site in the 1930s. As a selective institution it developed a reputation for being aggressively academic, and its roll call of past students included the first females to go on to graduate in law and medicine. Here, girls are put through an exercise regime in the school gym in the 1930s.

ABOVE: Renowned Australian photographer Harold Cazneaux took a series of photographs of the exclusive Frensham School for girls in the Southern Highlands of New South Wales in the mid-1930s. This picture, titled 'Oranges and Lemons', is a gentle portrait of a class of girls preparing for a festival.

RIGHT: High school retention rates for girls increased markedly from the 1970s. A number of factors contributed, including feminism, the availability of free tertiary places and climbing youth unemployment figures. Here, a 15-year-old Canberra girl studies at one of Australia's first open-plan high schools.

ABOVE: To be like Shirley Temple would have been a dream of many a little girl and her mother in the 1930s, which meant that Shirley Temple look-a-like competitions, such as this one held in Sydney in 1934, were ensured of a good turnout. Singer Gladys Moncrief, in her role of judge, complained that it was difficult to find a candidate with more than a couple of points of resemblance to the child star.

FACING PAGE: Providing girls with an education for the greater part of this century has meant having a bet each way. While it was important that the young ladies were versed in the academic fundamentals, it was of equal concern that they learnt the rudiments of home management. These girls are pictured at St Vincents Girls School in Sydney in the late 1950s modelling the frocks they had made in sewing class. Cooking, or domestic science as it became known, was also on the curriculum.

As the fortunes of the Australian colonies rose and fell, children were often the first to suffer serious deprivation and the last to recover. The Great Depression proved the frail nature of the safety net that had been put in place to protect society's most vulnerable. These small girls (**ABOVE**) were photographed in 1938 at the Havilah Orphanage in Wahroonga, New South Wales. Many other Australian childhoods were cut short by economic demands of the family or social expectations. Nina Christesen (**RIGHT**), of Brisbane, was by the age of 14 supporting her migrant Russian family by taking on jobs before and after school. On the western side of the continent, four-year-old Jennifer Cain (**FACING PAGE**) is busy at her 'work' in the wheat-belt country of Western Australia.

Images of post-war Australian childhood: The Lester family (**ABOVE**) of Devonport, Tasmania, is pictured in 1967 with their new Humber Vogue. Cars featured prominently in many family photographic records of the era. Debbie James (**LEFT**) plays at Surfers Paradise beach in the mid-1960s, when the Gold Coast was becoming the destination of choice for family holidays – the beachfront building frenzy was soon to begin.

ABOVE: While Australia and the West Indies battled it out at the MCG in January 1985, Bruce Postle captured this classic image of cricket at grassroots level: the Steenhuis family in Bungaree, Victoria, battling it out in a roadside paddock (including girls Donna, Maria and Lois).

Australian girls today can expect opportunities only dreamed of by their mothers and scarcely guessed at by their grandmothers. Girls have higher school retention rates than boys; they fill more than half the places at universities; and they are entering the workforce in almost equal numbers. Legislation enshrines their right to pursue these activities, while equal amounts of determination and impatience will hopefully see them overcome remaining discrimination. Here, three recent arrivals (**ABOVE**) enjoy a meal in Fitzroy, Melbourne; seven-year-old Tilda (**RIGHT**) tends to the needs of her Baby Born doll; and Natasha, aged eight (**FACING PAGE**), heads back out to the surf at Wye River, on the south-west coast of Victoria.

ABOVE: 'Quality time' is how families now describe the hours of leisure carved from chaotic schedules where, more often than not, both partners are wage-earners and where work no longer fits into a neat Monday-to-Friday timetable. The beach has been the overwhelmingly popular destination for generations of Australian families on holiday, and a cheap, convenient day out for the vast proportion of the nation's coast-clinging population. The 1990s family pictured here takes advantage of a broad expanse of sand for a moment of parent–child demarcation.

RIGHT: Keeping a family well turned-out has been a source of pride and pleasure, not to mention hard work, for many Australian women. Geraldine Ohlsson, pictured here in the late 1960s with her newly graduated husband, kept the family respectable, with only a student's scholarship as a family wage. With the help of the ubiquitous Singer sewing machine, she made the clothes that she and her children are wearing.

ABOVE: Washing day at the settlement of Lake Tyers in Victoria's Gippsland region, c.1900. Washing clothes was the most demanding of household tasks, and as soon as a housewife could afford to outsource some of her work, it was the local washerwoman to whom she turned. There was water to be collected and wood to be chopped. The clothes were boiled and stirred and then wrung out by hand. Crude appliances such as wringers and washboards helped only marginally.

LEFT: Carting water has long been women's work. Aid agencies working in Third World countries recognise this task as one of the most onerous placed on women, and often the first step in establishing a community is ensuring a permanent water supply. Before the advent of water tanks, wells, bores or a council water supply, Australian country women would carry water from wherever they could get it. The woman pictured here in a poor inner-city Melbourne suburb in the 1950s, carts water for her washing from her mother's house nearby; her water supply had been cut off for a week.

ABOVE: These young women of the Gippsland region, c.1920, are washing their 'smalls' in the local creek. A chat, a joke and the warm summer air help lighten the task.

RIGHT: Automatic washing machines, dryers and the ubiquitous Hills Hoist (or a Hills foldaway for those with little space) have made washing days virtually redundant. In modern times 'doing a load' is a matter of remembering to add the detergent. The downside is that we wash more clothes, more often, with a proportional increase in the tasks of hanging, drying and folding. This mother in Carlton, Melbourne, finds the washing basket a convenient place to leave her child while she dons her rubber gloves in order to tackle a bucket of nappies.

When prime ministerial hopeful John Hewson remarked in 1993 that he ironed his own shirts, a (female) commentator told him to come back when he was ironing his wife's shirts if he wanted a pat on the head. Such is the nature of ironing. In the pre-electricity and drip-dry days it was a thankless task, requiring women to stand next to the fire balancing a set of hot-irons, while pressing and starching the ornately frilled clothes and the heavily embroidered linen of the day. The lass manipulating the hot-iron (**RIGHT**) posed for this 1880s photograph, hence the sweat-free brow and cheerful appearance, while a woman from the country town of Drouin in Victoria (**FACING PAGE**) tests the heat, and a 1950s mother (**ABOVE**) in a spotless kitchen shares some ironing tips with her young daughter.

ABOVE: Less well-off women, particularly in rural areas, were often responsible for making clothes (including underwear) for the entire family, as well as curtains and linen. The tasks of sewing and mending were regarded with somewhat mixed feelings. On one hand, they represented more work at the end of a long list of chores; on the other, many women derived a good deal of creative pleasure from running up outfits that would ensure a well-turned-out family group. Equipping daughters with sewing skills was essential. Here Violet Trundle of Hughenden in Queensland keeps an eye on her daughter Ailsa, while running a garment through the Singer sometime in the 1920s.

LEFT: Kate, the wife of photographer J.W. Lindt, oversees the handiwork of her two sisters in the garden of their home, the Hermitage, c.1905. Wealthy women, who did not have the responsibility for making the family's clothes, used sewing for recreation and relaxation, concentrating their efforts on tasks such as fine embroidery and lacework.

ABOVE: Doris Oakrhind, photographed by her sister, the famous garden designer Edna Walling, is doing the mending by the afternoon light in the 1950s or 1960s. Many women had a mending basket that they would sit down with at night, or for a few quiet hours during the day.

ABOVE: Before the availability of a wide range of grocery items, the preparation of food represented an enormous commitment of time. There was an evening meal to prepare in an overheated kitchen that inevitably faced west; there was the constant stocking of pantries, boiling of preserves and baking of bread; and there was always the cleaning up. In this rare photograph of a 19th-century kitchen, the daughters of the house prepare a meal; one watches over the wood fire, one peels potatoes, one attends to a task by the sink and two others go about quiet tasks in the corner.

FACING PAGE: Jesse March, of Werrimull, Victoria, pictured in 1936, hangs a newly butchered carcass in the meat safe. The storing and preservation of meat, the staple of most diets, was an important part of country life in the hot, fly-ridden conditions of Australia.

ABOVE: The standard Anglo-Celtic fare that has dominated the Australian diet has been transformed by the different tastes and cooking techniques brought here by immigrants from Asia and Europe over the last half century. Here Caterina Di Mase makes ravioli in her kitchen in Carlton, a suburb that would become Melbourne's Little Italy during the 1950s and 1960s. As with other newly arrived groups, the women kept old cultures alive in a new country with the preparation of traditional food.

LEFT: Despite the wide availability of pre-prepared foods, many women still enjoy the creative challenge of turning raw ingredients into delicious meals; witness the enormous female consumption of cookbooks, television cooking shows and classes. Here a woman prepares a duck for stuffing to serve at a dinner party in country South Australia.

FACING PAGE: Despite the element of drudgery, cooking has its rewards. There have been the friendly bake-offs at country shows, the prized recipes and cooking tips handed down across generations, and the satisfaction of a well-laid spread. Photographer Ponch Hawkes took this image of her mother displaying a much-deserved sense of achievement over the Christmas lunch she has created.

ABOVE: In remote areas where there were no stores or the delivery of supplies was unreliable, the growing of produce was essential for survival. While men were out looking after the commercial farming interests of the property, women took responsibility for the kitchen garden and the livestock used to feed the household. Most families kept a few chooks for eggs and fresh meat, as with this woman in Nullawil in country Victoria, c.1915, posing for a photograph to be sent to her digger son in France.

LEFT: Fruit trees and vegetable plots were planted as soon as the house was built. In many areas, the scarcity of rain meant hand-watering the precious crops. Nothing was wasted. Vegetables and fruit not eaten immediately were preserved in a variety of ways and stored. In Werrimull South, Victoria, c.1936, a woman shows off her spectacular home-grown pumpkins, which were a popular choice due to their low water requirements.

FACING PAGE: Few people need to grow vegetables these days, but many are loath to let go of the satisfaction or savings that come with being a primary producer, no matter how small the scale. This resident of the Melbourne suburb of Kensington maintains an impressive country-style garden just minutes from the busy city centre.

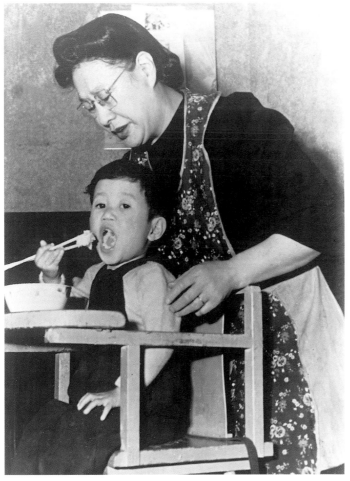

Alongside the endless lists of daily chores, there is usually the presence of children whose needs must also be attended to. It is difficult to imagine how the average 19th-century woman, who bore six to eight children, coped with both the physical rigours of housework and caring for young babies and toddlers. The fact that children grow, soon providing another pair of useful hands, was no doubt some compensation. Here a mother (**ABOVE**) prepares her children's weekly bath in 1905, and a child (**LEFT**) is fed in his highchair.

ABOVE: Many mothers of the outback have been proxy teachers to their children in areas where schools are too far away for daily travel. These children, pictured in the 1950s, are students of the School of the Air, a form of education allowing for classes to be transmitted via radio to remote districts. Since discipline was hard to administer across the airwaves, an adult, usually the mother, needed to be within close range of the learning process. Two-way radio was a lifesaver for many women, who could use it to chat to friends, receive medical advice and even 'attend' Country Women Association meetings.

ABOVE: Isolation, often identified as a difficulty for women from rural and suburban areas in modern times, plagued the lives of 19th and early 20th-century women in remote districts who had no adult females to converse with, let alone telephones or speedy mail deliveries. Letter writing to friends and family was a lifeline for many, and so prolific was the output and interesting the content that these letters and accompanying diaries have launched many a posthumous literary career. This rare 1860s photograph of a letter writer is attributed to Helen Elizabeth Lambeth and is part of an album titled 'Who and what we saw in the Antipodes'.

ROMANCE AND COMMITMENT

Life partners and close encounters

Within two weeks of the First Fleet's arrival, marriages were taking place in Australia. On 10 February 1788, 10 convicts were married. Among them were Mary and William Bryant, whose escape to Timor three years later with their two children captured the imagination of the British public and cemented the idea that the new colony was a place of adventure, danger and romance.

While weddings continued to occur sporadically, marriage was by no means commonplace. Of the 1430 adult women in the colony in 1806, only 395 were legally married. By the 1880s, however, about seven in every 1000 people were marrying each year, and three out of four adults were in 'respectable' unions. That figure has remained remarkably steady since, apart from a significant increase during the World War II years. What has changed is the traditional concept of marriage as a life-long commitment; and the increasing number of de facto relationships. In the 19th and early 20th centuries couples generally married for life; the majority of women had neither the inclination nor the means to leave their husbands. Although divorce legislation was introduced in 1857, successful applications were virtually unknown. In the 1990s
one-third of all marriages include one person who has been divorced compared to one in 10 in 1920.

Australians have celebrated their romances less than many nationalities. Within the arts, there have been exceptions, such as Frederick McCubbin's *The Pioneer*, C.J. Dennis' 'Washing Day' and Ted Egan's 'The Drover's Boy'. These works of art may not be overtly passionate, but they show an undeniable tenderness. Australians have been formal and restrained in few things, but they have tended to be exceptionally so in matters of romance.

FACING PAGE: When this Melbourne nurse married a senior resident medical officer of the Royal Melbourne Hospital in 1944, he was a Flight Lieutenant with the RAAF and about to depart for service in the Borneo campaign. Wartime weddings generally lacked ceremony and fashion; men wore uniform and the wedding service was often a simple ceremony at the registry office. Women from well-to-do families, however, could still indulge in the latest fashions. This photograph depicts the bridal party on the steps of the Toorak Presbyterian Church (now the Uniting Church).

ABOVE: This evocative study of a chance encounter at Fernshaw in the Dandenong Ranges near Melbourne in 1882 is one of the best-known images taken by renowned 19th-century photographer J.W. Lindt. For domestic servants of the period there was little opportunity to meet prospective suitors. Work hours were long and arduous, generally from 6am to 10pm, and in isolated communities social interaction was even more difficult. Although the German woman spoke no English and the male subject in the scene spoke no German, there is no mistaking the look of admiration in his steady gaze.

ABOVE: The story of actress Julia Mathews is one of ill-fated love. Her feelings for explorer Robert O'Hara Burke were so strong that she kept his image in a miniature around her neck. The pair planned to marry when he completed his crossing of the Australian continent in 1860–61, from which, of course, he did not return. After achieving success on the London stage in 1867, Julia Mathews died of illness less than a decade later, having never married.

ABOVE: A happier aspect of romance is depicted in this 1940s photograph of two sisters and their fiances in country Victoria. Both men had recently been demobilised from the RAAF.

ABOVE: Weddings in Victorian times were very much family affairs, as illustrated by this turnout of relatives in Tasmania in the 1860s.

ABOVE: Large numbers of German migrants settled in South Australia, fleeing political unrest in Europe in the 1840s. German communities with strong cultural ties were particularly evident in the Barossa Valley, and small towns such as Hahndorf, close to Adelaide. This typical German wedding, c.1900, has brought three generations together for the occasion.

ABOVE: In Victorian and Edwardian times weddings were traditionally all-white affairs and young flower girls and pageboys were popular inclusions in the bridal party. If fresh flowers were scarce, families improvised with the native flora, as in the bracken used in these wedding bouquets. This bride, flanked by her sister and husband, posed for the camera in Perth, c.1900–10.

FACING PAGE (ABOVE): On 10 December 1930 Mary Powell married world famous aviator Charles Kingsford Smith at Scots Church, Melbourne. He was to die only five years later when his plane crashed on a flight from England. Mary Powell was his second wife; he had divorced his first wife in 1929.

FACING PAGE (BELOW): Massie Pilven, a seamstress, of Footscray, married sweetheart Jack Myall, fitter and turner, of Yarraville, at St Georges Church, Footscray, in Melbourne's west in March 1934. The local newspaper reported that Massie had made her dress of silk net and blonde lace with a firmly tucked bodice, a skirt of tiny frills and a billowy veil of tulle, and for travelling she had chosen a brown ensemble with matching accessories.

ABOVE: In the last few decades women have taken a less traditional and subservient role at their own weddings. At this 1996 reception at the Museum of Contemporary Art in Sydney the bride, Heather Pearson, gives the speech while her husband listens from the sidelines. The service was conducted by a celebrant, a popular choice for couples today.

ABOVE: Captioned in the *Sunday Press*, 'The Hawks are home and hosed, but daughter Marilyn is still having difficulty getting father to the church', this delightful photograph by Melbourne press photographer John Lamb captured the bride's anxiety to get to her wedding ceremony on time, despite the efforts of father Ted to keep up with the football scores.

ABOVE: You are never too old to say 'I do'. Annie Wark, 90, and Alfred Harwood, 84, took the plunge at St Michael's, North Melbourne, in 1993.

Increasing numbers of modern-day couples wish to marry in a setting that offers natural beauty, such as a country, seaside or garden location. Bridget and Christo (TOP) took to the harbour in Sydney, the bride in a dress inspired by a 1920s Chanel creation. Melanie and Tom (ABOVE) decided on a quiet gathering of family and friends at the seaside resort of Lorne in 1995. There was a touch of old-world atmosphere in the ambience, with the bridal pair's attire evoking the romance of 1940s cinema. Jane and Colin (RIGHT), theatre director and actor respectively, decided on a medieval theme for their country wedding in Gippsland, Victoria, in 1995.

FACING PAGE: In the 1996 wedding service of Jacinta and Laurie, a combination of tradition and modern high style is evident. The Melkite Orthodox wedding ceremony is one of the oldest in the world and the two young people wore the traditional crowns. The bride's beautiful dress, however, was the height of contemporary fashion.

When Jeanette and Douglas Duffy (**ABOVE RIGHT**) went to Lorne for their honeymoon in 1944, the seaside town was little more than a row of stores, a couple of pubs and a collection of holiday shacks. It was wartime and holiday destinations were limited, but couples still carried on the tradition of some time away together. A generation later Lorne was one of the trendiest spots on the coast and Louise Campbell and Trevor Lemke (**ABOVE LEFT**), in the tradition of the 1960s hippie generation, found it an ideal place to be at one with nature.

LEFT: Sharing the good with the bad has always been part of a successful relationship. When the drought broke on their farm in Beveridge, Victoria, in 1930, Mrs Smith was as jubilant as her husband.

FACING PAGE: In the upright stance of Mr and Mrs Tim Nicholls from Gundagai, New South Wales, there is a pervading sense of compatibility and mutual respect, despite a life of pioneer struggle. When the passions of youth had mellowed and children had flown the coop, many 19th-century women faced a lonely and isolated future, often entrapped in a loveless marriage from which there was no escape. In rural communities elderly married couples were often bound by the ties of work, giving a form and purpose to their lives.

RIGHT: In the 200 years since white colonisation of Australia, there are a number of married couples who have won fame for their working contribution to the development of the nation. Marion Mahoney and Walter Burley Griffin, pictured at Castlecrag, Sydney, c.1930, were Chicago architects awarded the task of designing Canberra in 1912. After being stood over by a bureacratic officialdom, the Griffins moved from Canberra to Melbourne and later to Sydney. Although Mahoney's contribution has been less recognised than that of her husband, her landscaping and rendering are now widely lauded.

FACING PAGE: In 1928, Swedish-born poet and artist Ella Ström married Australia's most famous composer, the eccentric and flamboyant George Percy Grainger. Theirs was a shipboard romance, culminating in a wedding ceremony at the Hollywood Bowl (following a concert) in front of 20,000 people. The relationship was mutually beneficial, a rare combination of intimacy, companionship and professional understanding.

ABOVE: Ethel Dunlop Anderson married Stanley Bruce (Viscount) in 1913 at Sonning, Berkshire. She was his closest friend and confidant, and many of his decisions as prime minister (1923–1929) were made in consultation with her. Theirs was a union cemented by mutual interests – golf, bridge, motoring trips and the theatre. She had a great penchant for remembering names and faces, an invaluable asset on official engagements when she was always by her husband's side. When she died in March 1961 he was bereft and died a few months later. They are pictured here at the Lodge, Canberra, in 1928.

FACING PAGE: Politicians' wives 'suffer the slings and arrows of outrageous fortune' more than partners of most public figures. Tamie Fraser (ABOVE) always stood by her man. On this occasion the party faithful were celebrating the Liberal Party triumph in the 1980 election. Hazel Hawke (BELOW LEFT) was 'the woman behind the man behind the Labor government's re-election' in 1984. Felicity Kennett (BELOW RIGHT) has been affected more than most by her husband's position as state premier. She was forced to close her advertising business after media and opposition claims of a conflict of interest, and in 1998 she and husband Jeff separated for several months. When this photograph was taken, Kennett, then opposition leader, had just survived a leadership challenge and Felicity Kennett made the short trip to Melbourne's Parliament House to offer congratulations.

FACING PAGE: Modern marriage has witnessed the emergence of 'the sensitive new-age guy' and many relationships are testimony to the changing male–female roles. Men have become 'house husbands', taking on the domestic chores and child-minding duties that were for so long the traditional domain of women.

ABOVE: Since the sexual revolution of the 1960s, and the gay liberation movement that followed, same-sex couples have increasingly won acceptance. Legal recognition has been much slower; some states give same-sex couples equivalent rights to those of de facto heterosexual couples in property settlements, but homosexual marriage is yet to be recognised in Australia.

WORKING FOR WAGES

Struggling for equal opportunity and equal pay

In 19th-century Australia, women 's work meant homemaking and child rearing. When women sought work for wages, generally only under conditions of extreme financial distress, they found the jobs available largely demanded the skills held by any competent Victorian housewife, namely cooking, cleaning, sewing, child care, teaching and nursing. These 'womanly' areas of occupation were anything but gentle,' which is why as soon as circumstances allowed, married women paid someone else to do them. Women also began to fill the ranks of the nursing and teaching professions. They earned less than their male colleagues, but in recent times have received belated recognition for their contribution in developing health-care and education facilities that are regarded among the best in the world.

Employment opportunities began to expand for women in the early 20th century, but most of the work on offer was menial, in factories, offices and shops. Women rarely had careers, although a few courageously fought academic inequities to become Australia's first female doctors, lawyers and the like. Employment opportunities increased markedly during World War II but this progress was shortlived, and in the 1950s women were packed off back to their homes.

The impact of feminism since the 1970s has been profound. Laws that allowed women to be paid less than men, that prevented married women from being in the workforce, and that set limits on the types of jobs women could do have been swept away, to be replaced by powerful anti-discrimination legislation and affirmative action. Today, 43 per cent of the workforce is female and women's earnings are about 85 per cent of those of men. Subtle discrimination remains in the expectations of long working hours and the increasing cost of child care. It is no surprise that in areas such as politics, where night sittings are common, numbers of women are still disproportionately low.

FACING PAGE: Edna Walling (1897–1972) was the country's leading landscape designer in the 1920s. An English migrant, she arrived with her family in Australia about 1914. She dominated the garden world for four decades, writing a regular column in *Australian Home Beautiful* and four books. Her other passion, photography, gave her an added perspective on garden design, allowing her to more clearly view her trademark creations of winding paths, handcrafted stone walls, and gentle vistas of sweeping lawns and deciduous trees. Perhaps what is most remarkable about Walling is the extent to which she made her passion her profession in an era when work for women was most often driven by financial need.

ABOVE: When women moved into country and outback areas, living standards improved despite the humble nature of many dwellings. Housekeeper Mrs Donoghue lived and worked in this tent on a western New South Wales property belonging to James Connell, maintaining a remarkably well-equipped kitchen. Because of the labour-intensive nature of housework and the large number of children women bore, a maid was seen as a necessity rather than the luxury she is now. Often mistress and servant came from the same social milieu and had similar financial expectations. And often the mistress had been a maid herself, before being 'rescued' by marriage.

FACING PAGE: In 1901 about one worker in eight was employed in domestic service. In the early 1900s a maid was paid about £60 a year, a housemaid £40 and a parlour maid £50. Domestic servants worked long hours, generally from six in the morning until 10 in the evening. The indoor staff at the Como mansion in Melbourne included a parlourmaid, cooks, a housemaid, a needlewoman and a laundress.

ABOVE: In 1871 about one-fifth of New South Wales' children were educated at home, but within a decade that figure had halved. This was largely due to the introduction in 1872 of a state school system that made education compulsory in most colonies by the end of the 1880s. In rural areas, where access to schools was restricted, wealthy families employed governesses to educate their children. These women were often an integral part of the family, as depicted in this 1890s photograph in the Tilba Tilba district of New South Wales.

FACING PAGE: Here, Aboriginal maid Amelia Kunoth (1906) holds Edna Bradshaw, whose family was the first to occupy the Alice Springs Telegraph Station, located near the original springs after which the central Australian town was named. The telegraph line reached Darwin in 1872 and Alice Springs was just one of many repeater stations built along the line. Many Aborigines in outback Australia lived in virtual slavery, regarded as the property of their 'employer'. Others more fortunate became an indispensable part of family life. In both cases, traditions and culture were destroyed.

LEFT: With increasing numbers of women with children working outside the home, child care has become an issue for women across the whole spectrum of society. But with the cost of formal child care on the rise, relatives and friends are being recruited to help out. Here the grandmother pitches in so that the child's mother, seen returning home with the groceries, can continue with her job in a cafe. Women do the vast majority of unpaid work in the community, including looking after children and caring for the elderly.

ABOVE: Kindergarten mistresses at Cleveland Street Public School (New South Wales) in 1909 followed the principles laid down by German Friedrich Froebel (1782–1852), who thought children should be allowed to develop naturally, like 'flowers in the garden'. These days those who work in the kindergarten and child-care professions are still overwhelmingly females.

FACING PAGE: Colonial women wishing to become teachers could train at institutions such as the Model School, which opened in Melbourne in 1854. This mistress at a small ladies school at Preston in 1890 is pictured with some of her students, all well-dressed middle-class girls whose parents could afford the school fees. Private schools, subsidised by the government from the 1830s, lost their funding following the establishment of the state school system in the 1870s.

ABOVE: Established in London in 1878, the Salvation Army Corps set up branches in Sydney and Melbourne in late 1882. Founded on Christian principles, religious songs and brass bands were all part of the war against social evil. Condemned as rebel rousers by the established churches and public alike, the organisation gradually won acceptance by its increasing focus on social work. In more than 100 years of service, the 'Salvos' have established homes for the aged, the first in 1900, centres for alcoholics (from 1910), and in the 1970s taught English to Vietnamese refugees. For many decades Salvation Army workers, 'tin-rattlers', were a fixture in Australian pubs; the women workers seemed to have particular success in inducing men to donate some of their drinking money to charity.

LEFT: Cheryl Homes, a Mornington Peninsula hospital chaplain, and her husband were both ordained at the same time by the Archbishop of Melbourne, Keith Rayner, in 1995. Although the rate of entry into all religious vocations has been on the decline, there have been a significant number of women seeking to be ordained as priests, despite resistance from the churches, which have some sanction from Australia's normal anti-discrimination legislation. Homes is pictured here with sons Sebastian and Oliver, after her ordination as a deacon at St Paul's Cathedral.

ABOVE: Carmelite nuns in prayer at a convent in Kew, Melbourne, August 1980. The 13th-century order, after a period of obscurity, was revived in 16th-century Spain by St Teresa (1515–82), who founded the first convent of the Discalced Carmelites at Avila in 1562. The Carmelites today still wear traditional dress, dating from 1562, although footwear is now approved and a lighter habit has been adopted for summer. As an enclosed order their life is monastic, with days spent in contemplation and prayer. Holy days are observed with Gregorian chants and vespers sung in Latin. There are approximately 7300 Catholic nuns, from all orders, working in Australian today, although that number is steadily declining.

ABOVE: In the 1970s and 1980s, the air hostessing profession was given an ideological face-lift. Women with husbands and children were allowed to remain in their jobs; ideas on physical appearance became more flexible; and the influx of males into the profession helped speed up the change of name to flight attendant. But in the early 1960s, when this TAA air hostess welcomed an airline executive aboard a flight in Brisbane, the profession was yet to undergo its makeover.

FACING PAGE: During World War II the restrictions that were once applied to women's employment were swept away as men left and the nation experienced chronic labour shortages. Women answered the call, taking on work in a wide range of community, rural, military and industrial jobs, such as this Melbourne tram conductor, photographed in 1944. When the men came back from the war in 1945, women returned to the home, rather reluctantly in many cases.

ABOVE: Secretarial tuition was probably the most popular vocational training for teenage girls in the 1920s and 1930s. Pictured here are girls attending St Marys Commercial College, established in 1926 by Sydney's Sisters of Charity. The young ladies were trained in typing, shorthand, bookkeeping and personal presentation, and were highly sought after by the business community.

FACING PAGE: In 1908 a Grace Brothers magazine reported on women as a recognised force in the workplace. Whereas once their only options had been to become dressmakers, milliners, nurses, domestics or governesses, 'now, after years of repression and heaps of abuse, they have won their way into nearly every branch of business and most of the professions'. By 1918 office typists, such as this girl in Perth, were earning £130 a year for a 48-hour week.

ABOVE: At work in a Ballarat textile factory, Putu Suk Artini Sing proudly displays her Certificate of Australian Citizenship, which was granted on 7 June 1989. Born in 1962, Putu was one of thousands of Asian migrants to come to Australia in the wake of the Vietnam War.

RIGHT: In 1951 Australia and Italy agreed on the assisted migration of 9970 Italians by the end of 1952. By 1971 there were 290,000 Italian-born people in Australia and later in the decade they accounted for seven per cent of the population. Concetta D'Aloia, here at work in a clothing factory in Melbourne in 1956, was one of the many Italian women working in the textile industry during this post-war period. Such industries have absorbed large numbers of migrant women over the decades.

ABOVE: Pamela Skelton-Cox led the field for women in the very competitive industry of financial services and insurance. Born in Melbourne, she moved to Sydney in 1970, and became the first woman to be employed as an independent insurance advisor by the giant multinational insurance group Legal & General. She then went on to become the company's first female senior consultant in Australia. Working in the estate planning area in the days of death duties gave her a deep understanding of the vulnerability of families, and particularly women, who had not planned for the unexpected. In 1994 she won the prestigious W.W. Rodgers Agent of the Year Award, the highest honour that Legal & General (now Colonial) can bestow on any advisor, and she attends the company's annual conventions around the world, often as a guest speaker. Moving to Queensland in 1977, she established her own company in 1988 and now heads one of the leading insurance advisory, insurance brokerage and financial

planning firms in Brisbane, working closely with families, single women and corporations. Skelton-Cox is a strong advocate of financial independence for women and, apart from her professional interests, has been a tireless voluntary worker in the special events area to raise money for cancer research and handicapped children.

FACING PAGE: Gold was discovered in the Coolgardie area of Western Australia in 1892 and Kalgoorlie in 1893, leading to a gold rush that saw the population of the state increase by 400 per cent by the end of the century. Unlike many prospectors, goldfields' shopkeepers such as the intrepid Miss Murray and her assistant generally prospered. The social upheaval of the gold rush provided business opportunities for enterprising women.

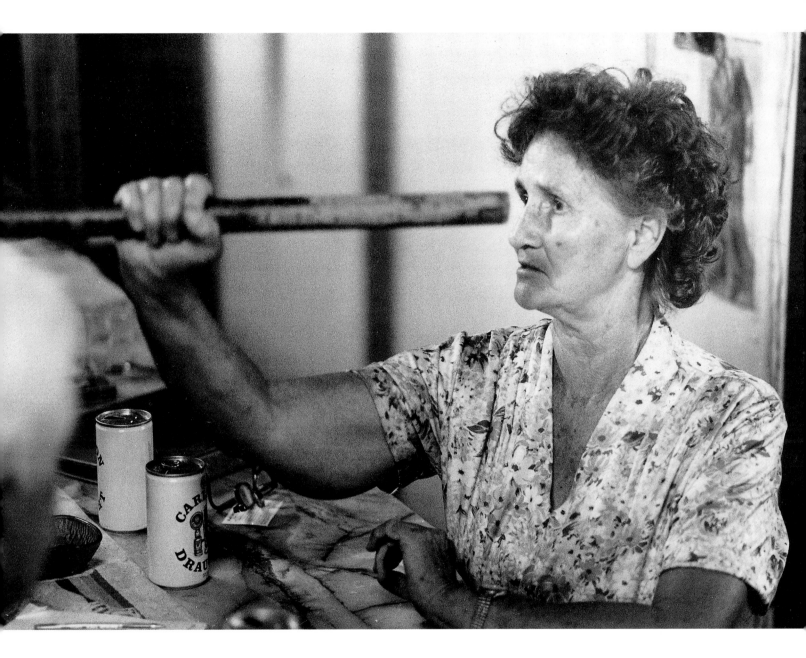

FACING PAGE: As a result of the powerful temperance lobby, barmaids were banned in some states in the early years of the 20th century, to prevent women from the corrupting influence of alcohol. South Australia introduced anti-barmaid laws in 1908, Victoria in 1916. Existing barmaids could remain but had to be registered, and female relatives of a hotel owner could be employed. The legislation was a failure – registrations were bought and sold and barmaids were still serving beers when the laws were repealed during World War II. In 1937, when this Sydney barmaid was working, the Depression had caused a massive slump in beer sales: in 1910 annual beer consumption per head was 27.5 gallons; in the 1930s it fell to 7.5 gallons.

ABOVE: Margaret Ellen Fairweather ran her pub (which was also a post office and general store) at Daly River, south of Darwin, from the late 1960s to the mid-1970s. The settlement, popular with fishing enthusiasts, is part of the large sweep of the Top End that still qualifies as frontier territory, and Fairweather was renowned for controlling outbursts of frontier-type behaviour with an iron fist.

ABOVE: These two field workers in country Victoria look as though they had never left their native Yugoslavia. The two Geelong women, hoeing a lettuce paddock in Werribee in October 1976, were bussed to and from nearby Geelong when their market garden employer was experiencing labour shortages.

FACING PAGE (ABOVE): For colonial breweries, supply of good-quality hops was always a problem. To cope with increasing beer consumption, 700 hectares of hops were planted in Victoria during 1883–84. In this early Bairnsdale photograph, all family members take part in the harvesting. Although rural Australia has had its own ways of discriminating against female labour, on thousands of farms one pair of hands is as good as another when it comes to the work that just won't wait.

FACING PAGE (BELOW): In the post-war years of the 1940s rabbit stew, although held in some disdain by the upper classes, was a popular dish in an era of general fresh food scarcity. Rabbits were imported into Australia by Thomas Austin of Barwon Park, Victoria, as sport for the squattocracy, and released into the wild in 1859. Within 30 years they reached epidemic proportions and for more than a century farmers have been trying to devise efficient extermination methods – from shooting, trapping and poisoning to barrier fencing, fumigation and biological control. Here, two women shooters display some of their catch during a rabbit plague in Northampton, Western Australia, in 1947.

ABOVE: Photographer Pat Holmes took this evocative shot of Lady Mountbatten's press conference in Canberra in 1946. The women who were busily recording her opinions were most likely correspondents from the now defunct women's pages of the daily newspapers, or from the country's stable of women's magazines. There have always been openings for women journalists in Australia, but for many years most had their talents forcibly channelled into the areas of fashion and soft news.

ABOVE: Doors began opening for female journalists in the 1970s and 1980s. One of the biggest changes was in the delivery and reporting of news on television, a task left traditionally to authoritative sounding men. Pictured here is young reporter, Jo Hall, on her first day on the job in 1980. Two decades later, as Channel Nine news anchor, Hall has demonstrated her ability to survive in an industry that has seen many women cast aside after being considered by the networks to have passed their use-by date.

LEFT: Journalist Maxine McKew won a Walkley Award in 1998 for her work on the ABC's prestigious interview show, 'Lateline'. Widely regarded as one of Australia's top journalists, she is seen here after an interview with US Secretary of State, Madeline Albright, and Secretary of Defense, William Cohen.

BOULIA
ourke River

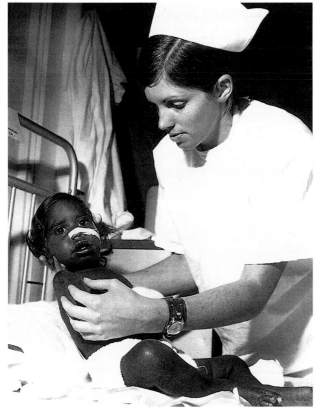

ABOVE: From the 1870s, many university courses admitted women, but some of the medical schools held off in case exposure to certain medical facts offended or overwhelmed female undergraduates. (The fact that women had been nurses since time immemorial seemed not to figure in this logic.) The University of Melbourne first admitted women into medicine in 1887, and in 1895 Margaret White became the first female to graduate. Another early graduate, Mabel Crutchfield, pictured here astride a camel, graduated in 1905, and then headed into the outback where she treated the ills of miners and their families in exchange for opals when cash was short.

LEFT: For more than 150 years successive governments ignored serious Aboriginal health issues. As late as the early 1970s, Aboriginal children, particularly in outback towns, were treated with discrimination. Here a nurse in Alice Springs cares for an Aboriginal child in hospital.

ABOVE: Nursing has always been a popular career choice for women in Australia. Today there are 175,000 nurses in the country and 88 per cent of these are women. Here, nurses graduate at the old Melbourne Hospital in the early 1940s.

RIGHT: Dr Heather Munro, pictured in 1997, is the first female President of the Royal Australian College of Obstetricians and Gynaecologists and a recipient of the Order of Australia. In 1888 the activist Louise Lawson complained about living in a society where babies were inevitably delivered by male doctors. Today children are still more likely to be coaxed into the world by a man: there are approximately 880 male obstetricians in Australia compared to 128 women. With trainees, however, the bias is reversed: there are 128 women compared to 88 men. This new, slight dominance of women training in obstetrics is mirrored in the other specialist areas and in the intake of medical students at universities.

PURSUIT OF PLEASURE

Fun, fashion and friendship

For women, who are said to do three-quarters of the world's work, the contemplation of a few hours away from toil and responsibility is particularly sweet. For the Australian battlers of the 19th century, who bore a child every other year and toiled with flat irons and coppers, the pursuit of pleasure was not high on the list of immediate concerns. Middle and upper-class women, those who could afford servants, fared better, although the problems of the household increased exponentially with size, and many women found that running a big household seemed to carry with it the same demands as running a small nation. But inevitably time was made, and Australian women began to identify the activities that suited them best. Friendships and accompanying social activities came first. Male mateship may be central to the idea of a national identity but women have always known who keeps the social wheels oiled, whether it is via a chat over the palings, or membership of a social club.

The kinds of activities that women have enjoyed over the years have remained remarkably constant, although clothing and general demeanour have changed dramatically. Australia's climate has given women the chance to get to the beach, out to the bush for a picnic, and onto a horse or a bicycle. Wearing fewer clothes for more months of the year than their sisters of the northern hemisphere, Australian women have made sure that leisure has also meant time for a bit of exercise.

Looking good, while not an obsession for most, has always been a concern. Many early photographs show immaculately attired women standing in front of the most poorly constructed homes, leaving the viewer wondering how such detailed grooming could have been achieved in such sorry circumstances. But perhaps that is what fashion, and indeed the pursuit of leisure generally, has traditionally been about for Australian women – the chance to beat fate, if only for a few hours now and then.

FACING PAGE: This photograph of sisters taking a stroll along the Puffing Billy train line at Emerald, Victoria, in 1948 is a captivating slice of 'Australiana'. The fashions easily identify the period. Jodhpurs then were an acceptable substitute for skirts (although pants were not), the head scarf was a popular accessory thanks to the influence of the Andrews Sisters, and the hand-knitted jumper recalls a time when few women would have entertained the thought of store-bought knitwear.

ABOVE: This young woman relaxes with a book somewhere in country Victoria around 1910, looking as much the reader as her rather formally attired male companions. Lack of access to education, isolation and the desire for some form of escapism traditionally made avid readers out of Australian women, and today they far outstrip men as book buyers and attendees of literary events.

ABOVE: Music was considered a necessary accomplishment for middle-class girls. While professional stage careers for women of this class were frowned upon, a wife who could enliven the home with some musical culture was a great asset. Mrs David Bruce, wife of the Clerk of Petty Sessions at Gundagai, was no doubt much in demand for her after-dinner renditions. She was captured at the piano in 1880 at the house of Dr Gabriel who, in addition to being the town's medic, was a talented and prolific amateur photographer.

FACING PAGE: Well into the 20th century the Chinese were systematically discriminated against in Australian society, causing the community to effectively withdraw in on itself. This was particularly the case for Chinese women who did not have business dealings by which to negotiate some access to the wider world. Home was where these women sought entertainment. An intimate evening, with some traditional music, surrounded by the rich accoutrements of one's own culture, would have been a pleasant way of shoring up against the strangeness of the society lying just beyond the front door.

ABOVE: Physical fitness was part of the routine for many modern
working girls of the 1930s. This rooftop workout is going on at
the Bjelke-Petersen School of Physical Culture in Sydney. The
fuller figure, popular in the earlier part of the century,
progressively 'faded away' during the 1920s and 1930s.
Organised exercise was one way for women to make sure that
they maintained the sleek line that fashion required. It was also
strengthening and invigorating, marking a final break with
Edwardian ideas on the fragility of the female form.

ABOVE: These women, from Sydney's Ice Follies, were getting downright daring in 1939, taking to skis in swimming costumes on the sand hills at Cronulla, New South Wales. Their bathers must have passed the test of the beach inspectors who, from the 1930s on, roamed the shoreline of Sydney measuring the bottom halves of the girls' two-piece swimming costumes to make sure they complied with the specified standards of decency.

No river, no swimming hole, but every farm had a dam, and Bubbles and Dorrie (**ABOVE**) were making the most of theirs on a property in the Mildura district of north-western Victoria, c.1925. Their swimwear is suitably modest for the times.
In contrast, the young women (**LEFT**) in Victoria's Gippsland region look remarkably modern.

ABOVE: Summer holidays in Australia are marred by a horrific number of drowning accidents and swimming has long been part of the school curriculum. These girls, from an exclusive Melbourne school, lined up to be photographed during a school training session in the 1970s. They are wearing their Speedos, the Australian standard in swimming attire, and the doll was an aid for teaching the techniques of mouth-to-mouth resuscitation.

RIGHT: Once restrictions on mixed bathing were lifted, Australian women found their place on the sand. The beach was one of the few public places in the early to mid-20th century where women could be comfortably alone or in the company of friends, as pictured here in the 1930s. On the right, Mrs Kavanagh of Irish origin and fair complexion, appears as something of a pioneer of the skin protection movement with her large hat and long-sleeved shirt – rare accessories in the days that heralded the start of Australia's great era of sun worship.

FACING PAGE: Australian pioneer women were remarkably intrepid and resilient. Irish-born Eliza Vievers arrived by ship in Brisbane as an immigrant girl in 1859, at the age of 17, and married Robert Vievers two years later. The couple made their way south in a sailing boat and settled near Nerang, 70 kilometres south of Brisbane. Photographed outside their crude slab hut in 1872, Eliza rides side-saddle and is buttoned up in tightly fitted bodice and flowing skirt, which must have been unbearable in the tropical heat. After Vievers' death she married a local farmer, but spent her last years in Brisbane. She died in 1929 at the age of 87.

ABOVE: Women riders have traditionally been a force to be reckoned with, professional or amateur, olympic entrant or outback jillaroo. This woman is a picture of cool confidence and total control as she steers her mount in the quarter-horse event at the Melton Rodeo, Victoria, in 1991.

ABOVE: Cycling for young women ballooned into craze proportions as a recreation at the end of the 19th century. These young ladies are out for a spin in Adelaide in 1896, on bikes not too dissimilar to those on the road today.

FACING PAGE: Women have a legendary capacity for coping with multiple tasks. In the late 1970s Yvonne Junghenn of Albert Park, Victoria, was photographed aboard her bicycle – getting some exercise while minding the baby, doing the shopping and walking the dog all at the same time.

FACING PAGE: After the deprivations of the war and immediate post-war years, the 1950s ushered in a period of growing optimism and prosperity. In 1954, when the young Queen Elizabeth II made the first visit to Australia by a reigning monarch, the population was predominantly white Anglo-Saxon and allegiance to the British Crown was still unquestioned. Men and women dressed up and lined the streets, here in Sydney, using every means available to get that magical glimpse of royalty.

ABOVE: A touch of sidewalk sophistication came to Melbourne in the 1960s and the 'Paris end' of Collins Street could have been the Via Veneto or the Champs Elysees, if one ignored that all too familiar rumble of the tram.

ABOVE: A work-related social occasion can bring revelations and a display of hitherto undreamed of skills and attributes. This floorshow by employees was a highlight of the McRae Knitting Mills ball at the Wentworth Hotel in Sydney in the 1950s.

ABOVE: Lofty surroundings and one of the premier scenic attractions in New South Wales, both then (1887) and now, is the Three Sisters rock formation at Katoomba. The three sisters in the foreground found their viewing platform a good place for a cup of tea, with proper cups and saucers. The Australian bush provided spectacular scenery and 19th-century city-bound women thought nothing of a trip to the mountains for a picnic, whether it was the Lamington Plateau in the Gold Coast hinterland, the Dandenong Ranges near Melbourne, or the Blue Mountains west of Sydney.

ABOVE: Where there is leisure and pleasure there is usually a cup of tea, refreshing, revivifying and just the thing for a break, a snack and a chat. These ladies at a country race meeting are enjoying a simple picnic on the grass.

SOCIAL TURMOIL

Life-shaping events of a nation

Women, traditionally, have not been the instigators of major social change, but in Australia they have certainly been active participants in the process. Eighteenth and 19th-century migrants endured the six-month journey out to Australia, often in deplorable conditions. They came as convicts, assisted immigrants or free agents. They attempted to carve a life for themselves and their families out of the rough and tumble of colonial towns, or headed into unknown territory to settle the land. Women endured all the same pioneering hardships as the men with whom they travelled, and bore and raised children, often without medical help. Just as they paused to take breath, gold was discovered and the rush that ensued was one of the most dramatic and socially disruptive events in the country's history. Women were left behind to hold home and hearth together, or accompanied husbands and encountered the most basic of living conditions.

In the 20th century women were once again left to fend for themselves and their children as two cataclysmic world wars exerted a claim on the nation's men. Some women joined the fight, signing up as nurses and witnessing many of the worst horrors of these bloody conflicts. During World War II women juggled personal sacrifice with a new-found independence. Many joined the forces as nurses or in a variety of technical, manual and intelligence roles; some ran factories and farms; and others tackled the onerous job of running homes and looking after children as single parents.

Post-war years have seen Australia open its doors to vast numbers of refugees and migrants, who have faced discrimination, dislocation and physical hardship. But the multiculturalism of the last decade, in particular, has also widened horizons, expanded career choices and instilled in women a greater strength of purpose than ever before in the last two centuries.

FACING PAGE: In 1918, at the end of the worst war the world had seen, these Sydney women waited for the return of their men from the killing fields of Europe. Out of a population of five million, 400,000 men enlisted and 60,000 were killed. This amounted to the loss of almost an entire generation of young men, leaving scarcely a wife or mother unscathed. The anxious young woman here clutches a box brownie camera.

ABOVE: On the recommendation of Quaker minister Edward Gibbon Wakefield, South Australia was created as a self-supporting colony of free settlers. There were to be no convicts; instead religious-minded individuals were encouraged to purchase land. In 1836 a group of 200 pioneers gathered at Glenelg beneath an ageing eucalypt to witness the governor's formal proclamation of the colony. Some six decades later, in the 1890s, this group assembled near the same spot to commemorate the success of Wakefield's experiment. Considering the grim determination and strength of purpose etched on these faces, it is little wonder that South Australia was the first Australian colony to introduce female suffrage.

FACING PAGE: The contribution of women in 'taming' the wilderness has often been overlooked. Whether they were assisted immigrants culled from the poor houses of Britain or the wives and daughters of middle-class men seeking opportunities, women shared the same hardships as their men, and often far more. Many travelled thousands of miles to their new homes, 'kept house' in tents and huts, gave birth without medical help, went for weeks without adult company when their husbands were away, educated their children, and pitched in when required with the heavy manual work of settling the land. Here a woman works alongside her husband on the back-breaking task of land clearing.

FACING PAGE: The gold rush, which swept through various regions of Australia between the 1850s and 1880s, has been described as having an effect on family life not dissimilar to that of war. As men threw in their jobs and headed for the goldfields, many women and children were left to fend for themselves in the cities. Occasionally, fathers and husbands were never sighted again. Some women followed their men to the goldfields, where they were outnumbered by four to one. Their presence was highly regarded – the degree to which women were trusted to look after men's earnings, which they carried in bags beneath their skirts, earned the acclamation that a woman was safer than a bank. Women, unlike men, were not required to have a licence to mine for gold, but only a few took advantage of the situation and struck out on their own, as in this rare photograph.

ABOVE: The gold rush presented women with unprecedented business opportunities. While in many cases this translated into activities such as prostitution and the running of sly grog shops, some did very well tending legitimate concerns, such as this storekeeper on the Gulgong goldfields of New South Wales, trading in basic supplies around 1872.

LEFT: A mother sends off her son, a member of the Australian Naval and Military Expeditionary Force, to fight in what will be Australia's first military engagement of World War I. Australian women became the focus of political attention in 1916 when a referendum was held on conscription. The prime minister, Billy Hughes, issued 'A Call to the Women of Australia' in the hope that women with sons and husbands abroad would vote to send back-up troops. Women were split on the issue. The majority did vote for conscription, but there were many who lined up with the socialists and pacifists in opposing it, including Vida Goldstein who, in 1915 proclaimed, 'The time has come when the women, the mothers of the world, shall refuse to give their sons as material for shot and shell'. The referendum failed.

FACING PAGE: When the first Australian nurses ever to serve in an overseas conflict arrived in South Africa in 1900, an English medic was reported to have said: 'My God, Australian sisters, what shall we do?' The first Australian nursing corps, the NSW Nursing Service Reserve, was established in 1898 by Nellie Gould, pictured here in 1902 with two of her team, recently returned from the Boer War.

LEFT: While the chance to serve one's country was a strong motivation for Australian nurses, the opportunity to travel was also very attractive, considering the restrictions normally placed on women's activities and their lack of independent means. During World War I, many more women applied than were accepted for positions overseas. Pictured here with their English and American counterparts are four Australian civilian-trained nurses, who served in a mobile hospital behind the lines on the Western Front in 1917.

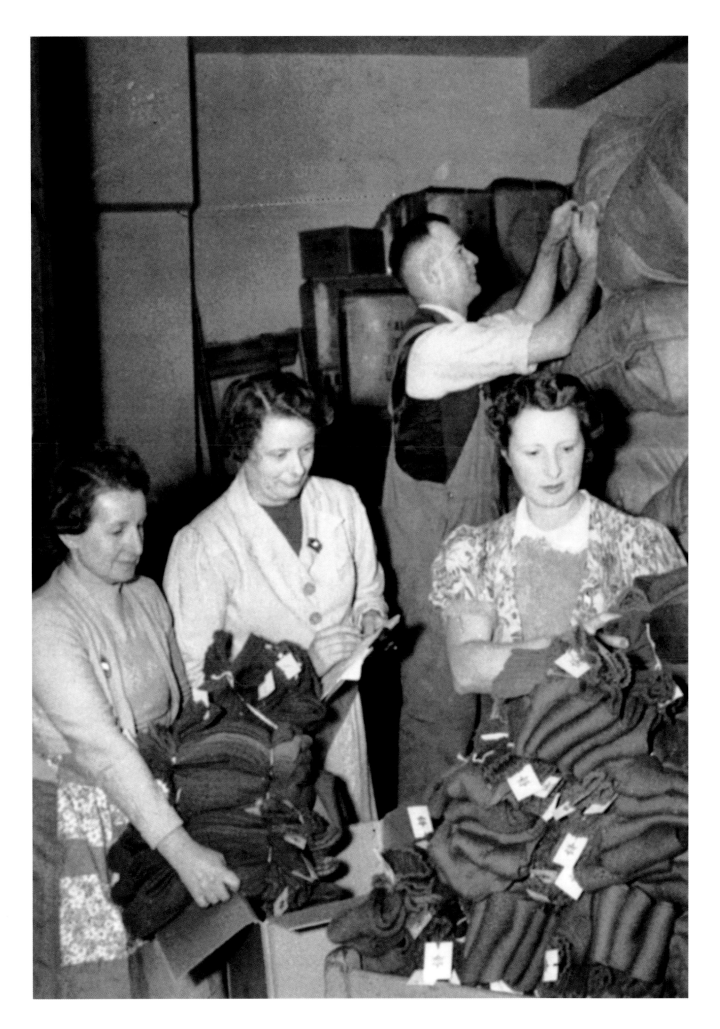

The work of the Australian Comforts Fund crossed the two world wars. A voluntary organisation, it made, packaged and sent off a variety of items, including food and clothing, which would provide comfort for the troops abroad. Women gathered in local shire and town halls across the country, gaining a strong sense of community and purpose. A sewing group (**ABOVE**) is photographed in the Melbourne Town Hall during World War I, and a generation later, Sydney women (**FACING PAGE**) sort out socks for World War II troops.

ABOVE: A nurse looks after children during an air raid drill at the Camberwell Babies Home in Melbourne in 1942. World War II was the only war that directly threatened Australia. With Darwin and other northern Australian towns attacked by Japanese aircraft and Sydney hit by midget submarines, Australia was on constant alert – a new experience for those left behind.

FACING PAGE: In another drill in the same year, women in Sydney take shelter in trenches. Many Sydney women and children, particularly those who lived near the Australian Naval Base at Garden Island, were evacuated to country areas.

ABOVE: Almost 4200 nurses served with the military during World War II, and 75 lost their lives in the line of duty. Those in the Pacific fared worst, with many dying from disease and starvation as Japanese POWs. Australian nurses were widely known for their courage and good humour. Highly respected war photographer Damien Parer recorded this group relaxing in the Northern Territory in 1942.

ABOVE: Australian troops fighting the Germans in Greece in 1941 were forced to retreat to the Thermopylae Line in April, before transshipping to Crete. The Germans carried out air attacks on this Mediterranean island in late May, forcing the evacuation of all Allied troops and personnel. This cemetery in Argos, Greece, provided refuge for these Australian nurses during an air raid in early 1941.

FACING PAGE (ABOVE): Damien Parer photographed these lonely figures farewelling the departing troop transport ship *Strathallan* in 1939. Women were expected to support the war effort and keep alive the idea of home for the troops. Advertising slogans blatantly encouraged them to look their best when their loved ones returned.

FACING PAGE (BELOW): The Australian Women's Army Service enlisted a large number of enthusiastic participants into a variety of areas, including military operations. With most able-bodied men in active service, women were trained in defence strategies. Here, an anti-aircraft gun crew use a height and range finder during an air raid exercise in Melbourne in 1942.

ABOVE: These women keep American troops on their toes at the Roosevelt Club in Kings Cross, Sydney. As the war dragged on many Australian women, missing entertainment and male company, turned to the thousands of US servicemen arriving on Australian soil. These troops, warmly welcomed at first, were to become the source of much hostility as they commandeered the affections of local females. 'Oversexed, overpaid and over here' was one of the more polite opinions expressed.

ABOVE: The ecstatic faces of these women say it all, as crowds gather in Swanston Street, Melbourne, to celebrate victory in the Pacific (VP Day) on 15 August 1945. The safe return of husbands and lovers from the six-year conflict was cause for rejoicing. Nevertheless, many women found the reality more difficult: returned servicemen, suffering physical and psychological problems, were not the same young men who had gone off to war, and some women found it hard to adjust to having a man back in their lives after being so long at the helm.

ABOVE: Max Dupain's famous photograph 'Meat Queue 1946', documents an aspect of the war years and post-war period that had a profound effect on civilians. Mothers, in particular, struggled as they tried to ensure their children were adequately fed, juggling a complex voucher system against a family's nutritional need. Rationing in Australia, while not nearly as severe as in Europe, still induced many to resort to the thriving and ruinously expensive black market to keep their cupboards stocked with the basics.

ABOVE: Army nurse Lieutenant Margaret Ahern carries a
Vietnamese baby in Hoa Long during the Vietnam War. Forty-
three Australian military nurses served in this conflict. Many of
these, like the soldiers, found it difficult to reintegrate into
civilian life after their experiences in what was to become the
most deeply divisive war in Australia's history.

ABOVE: War has been largely commemorated for the sacrifices made by men in combat. In the 1980s, at the height of feminist re-evaluation of historical events, women began to raise the issue of female sacrifice, focusing on the widespread rape of women by soldiers in wartime. Their protests were not met with much sympathy. But various world conflicts since, notably those in the Balkans, have shown that rape is not only something that occurs, but can in fact be part of military strategy. Seen here are women marching in Sydney on Anzac Day, 1983.

RIGHT: Debate continues on the place of women in the armed forces, with the more rigorous combat roles still off-limits. But as this picture of Corporal Julie Baranowski shows, things have come a long way since the time when the only military service available to females was nursing. Baranowski served with the Australian contingent to the Unified Task Force in Somalia in 1993, where being a woman proved a great advantage. Somali soldiers, hoping to avoid detection, would hide their weapons in women's clothing, knowing that male task force soldiers would be unable to conduct searches of the local women. Baranowski, of course, could search the women.

ABOVE: These would-be immigrants line up outside Australia House in London in the 1930s to find out more about what might become their new home. Arrivals from the British Isles accounted for approximately 75 per cent of the total immigration figure in pre-World War II Australia. By the late 1980s this figure had dropped to around 35 per cent.

RIGHT: This young Russian immigrant, Svetlana Logoothin, was the grand daughter of a Tsarist general. Her family and 200 other Russian families lived in hessian shacks on cotton farms in Biloela, Queensland.

FACING PAGE: Wong Kwei Far (pictured here with daughter Ida) was the fourth wife of Kwong Sue Duk, a herbalist who set up shop in Cairns in the early 1900s. Kwong had four wives, including three in Australia, and fathered 26 children. One of the few Chinese to practise polygamy in Australia, he was not condemned by the remote northern community for his ways. His wives may well have derived comfort from their number, given that contact with the European sector of the town was virtually non-existent.

ABOVE: Before World War II, many southern European men came to Australia to get established before sending for their wives and children. Sometimes the separation of families was for a short period only, but it was not uncommon for years to pass before men, women and children were reunited. Here an Italian mother and her offspring await the call from Australia.

During the years directly following World War II, Australia saw a dramatic change in the make-up of its migrant population. Between 1947 and 1954 a quarter of a million displaced persons from war-ravaged European nations (other than Britain) were resettled here, representing around half the total immigration figure. A group of Jewish immigrants (**ABOVE**) begin their long journey, arriving to settle in a new land; and former displaced men, women and children of the Baltic region (**RIGHT**) settle down to a meal at Seymour railway station in Victoria in 1947, en route to the migrant camp at Bonegilla in the state's north-east.

FACING PAGE (ABOVE): The Chinese have a long history of immigration to Australia. Today Chinese Australians account for about 1.2 per cent of the population, a figure disproportionate to their significant contribution to the community. Pictured in 1987 is Chee Kin Chew, proprietor of Victoria's first nursing home for Chinese, and three of his residents.

FACING PAGE (BELOW): Muslim women attend a class in Melbourne in the 1990s. The first immigrants of the Islamic faith to arrive in Australia were camel handlers, who worked in South Australia during the construction days of the Overland Telegraph Line in the 1870s. Few women accompanied these men, but intermarriage with European settlers was not uncommon. Today there are around 200,800 Australian Muslims, representing the largest non-Christian religious group in the country. Many hail from the Middle East and southern Europe, but increasing numbers are arriving from African and Asian nations.

ABOVE: Jun Won, 94, and Luu Thi Van, 84, enjoy a meal at the Victorian Elderly Chinese Welfare Society clubrooms. The traditional Chinese food was subsidised by the Melbourne City Council and organised by Meals on Wheels. The arrangement recognised that the English-style fare normally offered was not necessarily to everyone's taste in a society as diverse as Australia.

ABOVE: Newborn Maximilian Starkowski sleeps safe and sound flanked by four generations of his female relatives, unaware that his presence represents a crucial chapter of Australia's post-war history. Great-grandmother Helene Trybusc (far left) came to Australia with her husband in 1949 from a displaced person's camp in Germany. Without money or possessions, they started their Australian life in a migrant camp working as farm labourers. Helene brought her mother, the baby's great great grandmother, Janina Kuchta (centre left), and her father to Australia in 1951. Helene's daughter Wanda Zebrowski (centre right) married a statistician and set up house, and Maximilian's mother, Jola Starkowski (right), is a graduate in behavourial science.

FACING PAGE: Yen Pham, one of 10 children whose father had been 're-educated' because of his support of the overthrown South Vietnamese government, left Danang in Central Vietnam in 1982 as a 21 year old. After a period in a Hong Kong refugee camp, she resettled in Melbourne, finding a job in the Dead Letter Office. Suffering extreme hardships along the way, her parents and siblings gradually followed, the last arriving in 1997. While earning a masters degree, Yen supported her family, which now includes a doctor, dentist, engineer, architect and computer scientist. She is pictured here (far left) with her parents, siblings and their children outside her Yarraville home.

AGAINST THE ODDS

Hard times, good times, survivors and heroines

Henry Lawson's classic tale, 'The Drover's Wife', provides a powerful image in Australian folklore: a woman waiting stoically for her husband to return, all the while running the farm, fighting the elements and raising the children. So often in our history, women's resilience has been called upon because of the absence of their men, whether droving, digging for gold, searching for work or fighting a war on foreign soil.

The destructive force of nature has always been a powerful determiner of the Australian character. Floods, bush fires, droughts and cyclones have all regularly ravaged Australian communities, threatening and destroying the homes that people have worked so hard to create. Photographs of these events are evidence of the ability of Australian women and men to literally pick up the pieces and start again.

Natural disasters have often been compounded by the threat or reality of poverty. While both sexes have suffered, it has often been the women, with reduced employment opportunities and children to care for, who have felt the hardship most profoundly. Their resilience in such circumstances has been about protecting the rights of their families to a home, food and other basic needs, and their right to engage fully in life on this unpredictable continent.

Women have also shown an adventurous spirit and a willingness to accept life's challenges, such as sailing solo around the world, crossing the continent on a camel or running a property or business corporation after a husband has died. In the final analysis, fighting the odds has been a salient feature of Australian life.

FACING PAGE: Ellen Quinn, of Belfast, was a petite nine year old when she arrived in 1841 on what is now Port Melbourne beach, when Melbourne was a fledgling colony. Eight years later she would meet and marry ex-convict Red Kelly and together they would produce a clan that would leave an indelible impression on Australia's national character. Her family would face constant run-ins with the law; she would be gaoled herself. She would lose sons Ned and Dan initially to bushranging and finally to death in 1880. The indomitable matriarch lived until 1923 and is pictured here in 1911, with grand daughters Lil and Alice Knight.

FACING PAGE: Mary Nye was happily married to a farm labourer in England when he was arrested, convicted and eventually transported to Van Diemens Land. His crime was to be in possession of an egg for which he could not satisfactorily account. Determined to follow him, Mary committed a similarly minor offence and was also transported to Van Diemens Land. But her husband had disappeared and Mary never saw him again.

ABOVE: Pacific Islanders work on a Queensland cane plantation in the 1870s. Men and women Kanakas, as they were called, were often lured from their homeland by unscrupulous labour contractors – a process called 'blackbirding', which was little better than kidnapping. The system lasted from 1863 until 1906. The cane workers were supposed to receive 10 shillings a month, but this was often paid in kind, namely with an allowance of tobacco and a supply of clothing. Many died of diseases such as tuberculosis and others were subjected to appalling human rights abuses. Federation in 1901 brought with it the 'White Australia' policy and prompted the *Pacific Islander Labourers Act*, which required the deportation of Kanakas by 1906. Only those who had lived in the country for 20 years or had married or owned property were allowed to stay.

The ability of many women to create a home despite difficult
circumstances is a common thread linking Australia's colonial
days to its more recent history. Pioneers, diggers, the poor of
the inner cities and post-war settler farmers all faced a range of
hardships from stifling heat or freezing temperatures to lack of
water or firewood. Here a mother and daughter (**ABOVE**) stand
outside their miner's cottage in Lithgow, New South Wales,
during the late 19th century. In South Gippsland, Victoria, the
Penny family (**FACING PAGE**) lived in this burnt-out tree for nine
months in 1906. The tree house was six metres across at floor
level and had room for a double bed and a three-quarter bed.
The Pennys went on to build two houses, a butcher's shop, a
general store and a boarding house.

It is women who tend to suffer most when social safety nets do not exist. Those elderly women of the 19th century who had no families to rely on often found themselves in dire financial circumstances despite a life of hard work, raising families, making homes and contributing to pioneer communities. Here an elderly woman (**FACING PAGE**) sits in the sun outside her humble cottage in Sydney. In 1901 applicants for old-age pensions (**RIGHT**) wait their turn at the City Court in Melbourne. Also in Melbourne almost 90 years later, a 68-year-old homeless woman (**ABOVE**) moves through a bitterly cold morning. Homelessness, a tragic circumstance seldom seen in the prosperous days of the 1950s and 1960s, is becoming increasingly evident in Australia.

ABOVE: In Tasmania, as in many areas of colonial Australia, the best land was incorporated in large holdings owned by the wealthy. Surrounding these properties were many small landholders, struggling to make a living from poor, rocky ground. In times of depression, such battlers were hit the hardest. The Pearson family of Ouse, a town in the midlands of Tasmania, was photographed in the 1930s.

ABOVE: Two smiling women at Happy Valley during the 1930s. Happy Valley was a shanty settlement that sprang up south of Sydney. Its residents, many middle-class victims of the Depression, set out to prove that a positive, healthy outlook was still possible despite their dire financial circumstances.

ABOVE: A meal in a Redfern terrace, 1938. Redfern, an inner-city suburb of Sydney, became the focus of national attention in the 1970s when attempts were made to evict residents, many Aboriginal, from dilapidated dwellings to make way for new developments. Restoration of some of the public housing resulted. Sections of the suburb are now highly prized for their real estate value.

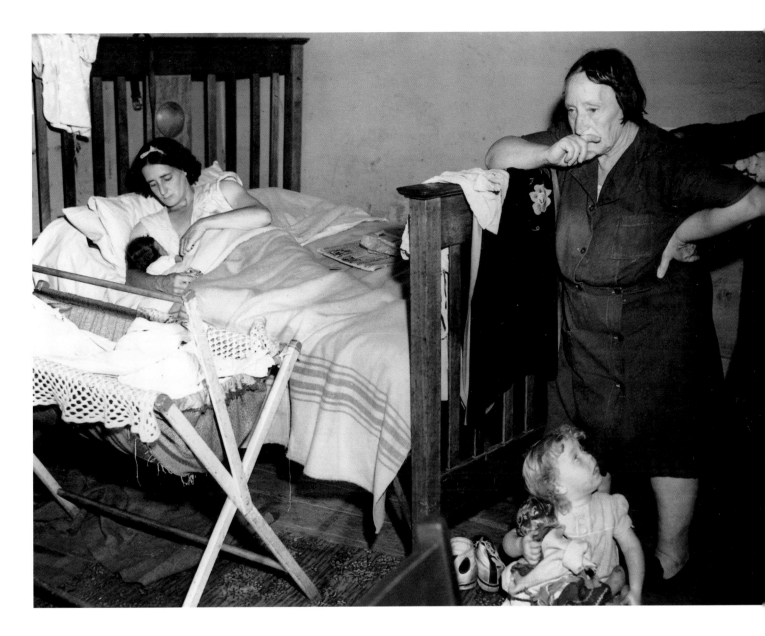

ABOVE: Photographer David Moore, who worked for Max Dupain for a time, took this haunting image of a family facing eviction from their Redfern home in 1949. As unemployment in Australia skyrocketed from 9.3 per cent in 1929 to at least 35 per cent in 1932, eviction became commonplace as families were no longer able to pay their rent. Men may have considered themselves failures as breadwinners, but for women eviction was a symbol of their failure as homemakers. As the Depression continued, eviction prompted community anger and despair, with resistance groups springing up in many neighbourhoods.

ABOVE: Jan Elward sifts through remnants at a friend's home after fires swept through Ferny Creek in the Dandenongs, just outside Melbourne, in January 1997.

RIGHT: A Tasmanian couple's home explodes in flames in bush fires that killed more than 50 people and destroyed many hundreds of homes on 7 February 1967.

FACING PAGE: In November 1968 Mrs Ereitkreutz, of Killarney, in south-east Queensland, told reporters how she had been serving the family dinner just before 8pm when a tornado destroyed her dining room. She did not know whether to laugh or cry when the press cameraman photographed her among the rubble.

ABOVE: Cyclone Tracy hit Darwin early on Christmas Day, 1974. Winds of 300 kilometres an hour flattened the city, killing 50 people and displacing half the residents. Those whose homes did survive faced the daunting task of cleaning up and re-establishing their lives in a largely abandoned city.

FACING PAGE: Marilyn Peacock sits in her flooded kitchen in Yeronga West during the Brisbane Australia Day flood of 1974. When the waters subsided the worst aspect was the appalling stench of mud that pervaded the devasted homes. The Queensland city has been ravaged by floodwaters several times in its history, the worst in 1893 when the Victoria and Indooroopilly bridges were completely washed away. The 1974 disaster inundated 14,000 homes and killed 14 people.

ABOVE: Vivian Bullwinkel trained as a nurse in Broken Hill, before joining the Australian Army Nursing Service during World War II. On her way to serve in Malaya in 1942, her ship *Vyner Brooke* was bombed. As she and 21 other Australian nurses reached the beach of Banka Island, they were machine-gunned by Japanese soldiers. Bullwinkel was the only survivor, hiding in the jungle for 10 days before being recaptured. She spent the rest of the war as a POW. She survived by telling herself repeatedly 'all I want to do is to get back amongst my own people, I don't care how long I'm taken prisoner'. She is seen here with her mother in October 1945 at a reception in Heidelberg, Melbourne, held

to honour nurses who had been POWs. Bullwinkel went on to win the 1947 Florence Nightingale Medal and became the first female trustee of the Australian War Memorial.

FACING PAGE: Juanita Nielsen disappeared on 4 July 1975 when she was editor of an inner-city Sydney newspaper *Now*, which campaigned heavily against development that would destroy historic houses in Kings Cross, and against the powerful, sometimes allegedly criminal, interests at stake. The prevalent theory is that she is buried under one of the apartment blocks she opposed.

LEFT: Lindy Chamberlain's resilience is unparalleled: she was accused of killing her 10-week-old baby despite her constant protestations of innocence; she faced a trial by media that lasted much longer than her legal one; and she spent five years in prison before her conviction was quashed. The events, played out in the 1980s, captured the imagination of the nation. Laden with metaphors of lost babies, wild animals, a desert environment, unconventional religious belief, and a mother who refused to display her grief for the benefit of the marauding media, the case became the biggest the nation had ever seen, while Chamberlain emerged as the most savagely judged woman of her time. She is pictured here on the media trail in 1990, promoting the release of her autobiography, *Through My Eyes*.

LEFT: Sara Henderson took over the running of an enormous cattle station, Bullo River, after the death of her husband, Charles, in 1986. She was named Qantas/Bulletin Business-woman of the Year in 1991 for her efforts and *From Strength to Strength*, the first in a series of best-selling autobiographies, was named Australian Book of the Year in 1994. In total her books have sold well over one million copies worldwide.

FACING PAGE: Young Australian woman, Robyn Davidson, had a dream of travelling alone halfway across the continent, from desert-bound Alice Springs to the Indian Ocean in Western Australia. She learnt desert sense from an Aboriginal elder and camel handling from an Afghan camel trainer. In her best-selling book *Tracks* she recounted her epic journey to a fascinated nation. Explaining why she didn't ride the camels more on the 2700-kilometre journey, she wrote: 'Although feet can get very painful, bums can suffer even more'.

PUBLIC LIVES, PUBLIC DEEDS

Activists, campaigners and the strong of spirit

When Joan Kirner became premier of Victoria, her elevation to the top job was described simply: from mother's club to premier. Women were rare is such positions. A cartoonist drew the premier in curlers and a spotted dress and, when confronted by Kirner as to why he persisted with the caricature, he confessed that 'He had never before had to draw a woman in power and he had no idea how to do it'.

Women have always played a part in public life, but until recently Australian females were not born to rule. It is scarcely 80 years since the first woman won a seat in an Australian parliament. While men have made public life and recognition a goal, for women, the attainment of both has been something of an accident; often a byproduct of their activism. Kirner did not want to send her children into overcrowded classrooms; Australia's first parliamentarian, Edith Cowan, wanted to protect women and children from the terrible events she herself had experienced as a child; and Mary MacKillop wanted to establish an institution to care for the poor. Public life, political career and power were not the motivating forces: it was the desire for change and social reform.

For contemporary women, a role in public life is something that can be planned for and realistically achieved. Women, like men, can and do support causes to advance their profile, rather than the reverse. But for many, the cause is still the important factor, and women continue to show a strong inclination to work for communal good rather than personal gain. This is particularly the case with grassroots activism, where women, working anonymously for change and reform, are making a significant contribution.

FACING PAGE: An elderly demonstrator protests against a rise in the price of stamps at the GPO in Bourke Street, Melbourne.

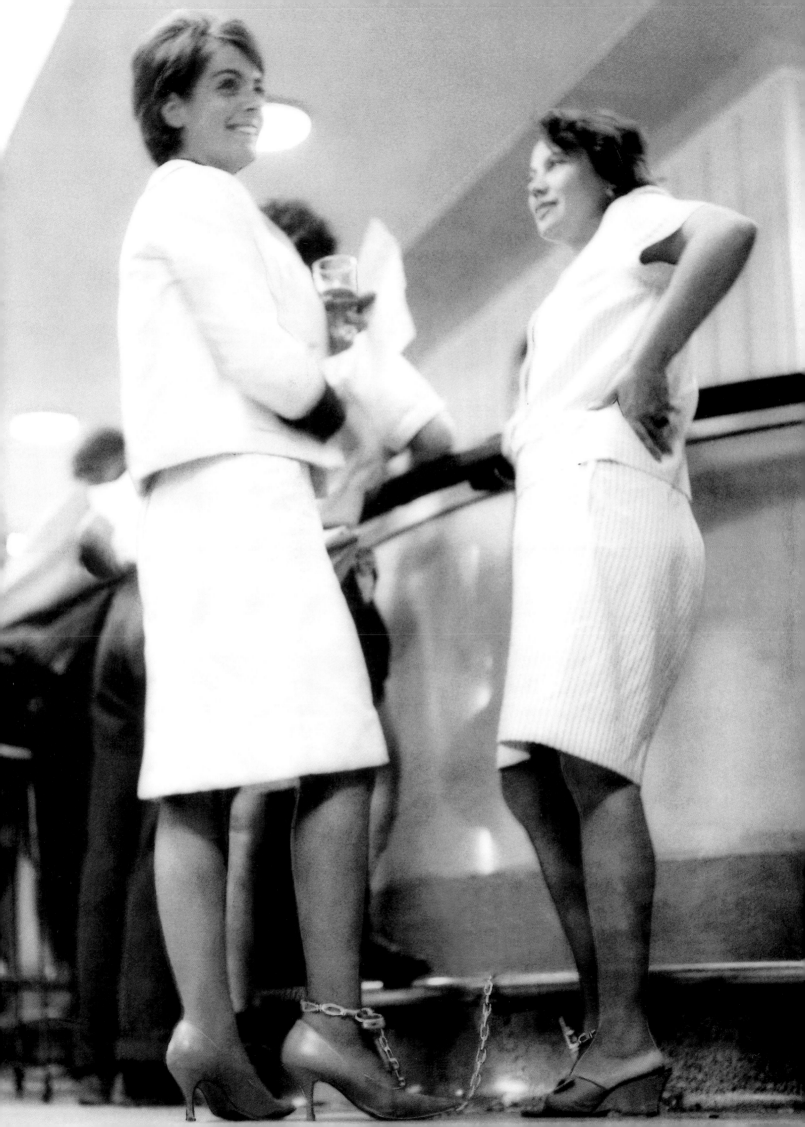

From its earliest colonial days, Australia has produced women who were not prepared to play by the rules. Fame for these women has meant both derision and celebration, and their place in Australian history undergoes regular revision. Daisy Bates (**FACING PAGE**), born in Ireland in 1863, was considered an eccentric, always dressing formally in a long skirt, high-necked shirt and gloves and living alone with Aboriginal people for extended periods of time. She documented a number of Aboriginal languages and her writings highlighted inadequacies in Aboriginal welfare. But her major work, *The Passing of the Aborigines*, encouraged the view that Aboriginal people were doomed and her 'scientific' methods are now dismissed. Germaine Greer (**RIGHT**), Australia's best-known feminist and academic, shot to international fame in 1969 with the publication of *The Female Eunuch*, which shocked some but was heralded by others as the bible of the women's movement. Her subsequent books and academic studies have been greeted with less public hysteria, but have nonetheless expressed her commitment to openly question female roles in Western societies. Blessed Mary MacKillop (**BELOW**), who was excommunicated for a period from the Catholic Church in the early 1870s, may one day become Australia's first saint. The order she founded, Sisters of St Joseph of the Sacred Heart, is still committed to helping the poor.

ABOVE: In May 1975, beneath the frowning countenance of Queen Victoria, a group of young people protest against hospital abortions at the old Queen Victoria Hospital. Contraception and abortion were major issues in the late 1960s and early 1970s. The Right to Life movement emerged in Australia during that period, using often intrusive means to try to prevent abortion and, more recently, euthanasia legalisation. But the violence that has marked the abortion debate in the United States has been absent here.

FACING PAGE: Every year the annual opening of the duck-shooting season is accompanied by graphic photographs of protesters holding dead and injured birds. This woman, part of a small group organised by animal liberationist Laurie Levy, was out at dawn on Lake Buloke near Donald, north-west Victoria, in March 1991. Largely due to the efforts of such groups, the duck season has been considerably shortened.

Senator Cheryl Kernot (**ABOVE**), seen here on the campaign trail in Melbourne during a Williamstown by-election in 1994, caused shockwaves when in 1997 she abandoned the Australian Democrats, which she had led for four years, to join the ALP and subsequently its frontbench. Following her departure, Natasha Stott Despoja (**ABOVE RIGHT**) became deputy leader of the Democrats. She had been elected to the Australian Senate in 1995, as a 26 year old. In the prolonged negotiations over the GST in 1999 she has stood by her principles, defying her party leader and declaring that she will cross the floor and exercise a conscience vote against the Bill, to keep faith with her election promise.

RIGHT: Amanda Vanstone has been a senator for South Australia since 1984 and Minister for Justice in the Howard government since 1997. She is the best-known woman in federal Liberal politics, partly because of the seniority that has come with her various portfolios (Employment and Justice), and partly because of her forthright manner. This attribute, along with a well-developed sense of humour, has earned her a great deal of respect.

FACING PAGE: Sonia McMahon caused a sensation in this dress when she appeared with husband Billy on his election to Prime Minister in 1971. Like many political wives in Australia her influence on her hsuband was significant, and her high profile was important to his career.

ABOVE: Admitted to the New South Wales Bar in 1955, Elizabeth Evatt's career highlights include serving as president of the Australian Law Reform Commission and chief judge of the Family Court of Australia. She has served on the United Nations Human Rights Committee since 1993 and the Human Rights and Equal Opportunity Commission since 1995.

RIGHT: Mary Gaudron was appointed to the High Court in February 1987. A Queen's Counsel since 1981, she was previously Solicitor-General of New South Wales. She served as Deputy President of the Australian Conciliation and Arbitration Commission from 1974 to 1980 and was appointed the first chairperson of the Legal Services Commission of New South Wales in 1979.

ABOVE: Dame Roma Mitchell, born in 1913, was Australia's first woman Queen's Counsel (1962), the first woman judge of the Supreme Court (1965), and the first woman state governor (South Australia, 1991). She is shown here in action, representing the Bar at a retirement occasion, c.1970.

Non-violent action, a form of protest that became popular during the Franklin River blockade in Tasmania in the early 1980s, has encouraged more women with children to join environmental protests. Each summer, many spend weeks and even months living in camps attempting to save wilderness areas across Australia. Near Omeo in north-east Victoria, this group (**ABOVE**) were campaigning against the logging of the area's old-growth forests. Non-violent action of a different nature, this centenarian (**FACING PAGE**) demonstrates for her right to respect.

RIGHT: Dale Spender, activist and intellectual, has for the last 20 years been there to alert us to the subtle and not-so-subtle methods of sexual discrimination. She started out with a PhD that looked at the way men and women communicate, and concluded that 'Not enough women were talking – it looked as though I was going to have to do a PhD on women saying "Mmm…uhhuh…mmm…really?" while men talked and talked'. Among her 30 or so books, she has delved into the previously unexplored area of women's contribution of Australian literature, and most recently has ventured into the brave new world of information technology with *Nattering on the Net*, a book about women and the Internet.

Age is mostly
a matter of mind —
if you don't mind
it doesn't matter.

FAIR PLAY

Professional, amateur and recreational sport

Australia has been producing female sporting champions for more than a hundred years. This concentration of talent is variously attributed to diet, climate, environment, genetics and the development of a sports-mad culture from which women, in many sports, have not been excluded. In the photographs of the well-to-do settling in for a seemingly benign game of croquet or lawn bowls, a fiercely competitive glint can be seen in many a Victorian matron's eye. Other 19th and early 20th-century photographs depict determined lasses who, despite neurotic predictions of gynaecological disasters, insisted on pursuing 'unsuitable' sports such as competition swimming, cricket and even football.

In the 1920s and 1930s fashions became freer and exercise more important, and attitudes to the physical capabilities of women relaxed considerably. The World War II years, when women did men's work on the factory floor, on the farm and in the armed services, saw the final overhaul of ideas on what women could physically achieve. And in the 1950s, the rise of the likes of Betty Cuthbert, Dawn Fraser and Marjorie Jackson put the final touches to the picture that was emerging of Australian women as sporting champions in their own right.

Since then there has been no pause in the pursuit of sporting excellence among women. We count among our number record breaking world champion swimmers, a couple of graceful and successful tennis players, a golfer who seems to be redefining the game and track and field athletes who apparently never reach the edge of their reserves. In addition there are the awesomely successful hockey ands netball teams, and the hundreds of thousands of casual and amateur sportswomen who troop off to netball courts, swimming pools and ovals each weekend with a measure of the same determination that drives those at the very top of their field.

FACING PAGE: Emma George personifies the dynamic nature of female sport in Australia, captured here by Melbourne press photographer Bruce Postle in February 1997. George is bright, focused, fit and possessed of enormous athletic talent. Arms raised in triumph, she is seen breaking a world women's pole vault record at an international sports meeting at Olympic Park, Melbourne. Since then she has gone on to break her own record several times, pushing the bar higher and higher in this relatively new international event for women.

ABOVE: Medical and social opinion was against strenuous exercise for women in the 19th century, so croquet, requiring very little exertion, was deemed an appropriate sport for the ladies of the leisured classes. It also suited the fashions of the time, which included fancy hats, breath-defying corsets and voluminous skirts. But croquet was also a game of fierce rivalry, and the female participants no doubt enjoyed the chance to exercise the competitive streak they supposedly did not possess.

LEFT: Ms Lilly Bradbury pads up at the Collingwood Social Club picnic in 1922. For most women, cricket entailed the occasional light-hearted swing at the ball on a beach or picnic; they were far more likely to be spectators at this popular game of the Empire. However, women's cricket teams did exist (the first recorded match in Australia was in Bendigo in 1874) and the sport has developed into active district and state competitions, as well as an international Test series. The fact that these events attract nothing like the press coverage given to men's cricket is indicative of the lack of attention given to women's team sports generally.

FACING PAGE: Traralgon housewife Lynn Crawford invaded a conventionally male domain by qualifying as an umpire for the Central Gippsland Cricket Association in eastern Victoria. Her primary motive was to keep fit during her pregnancy.

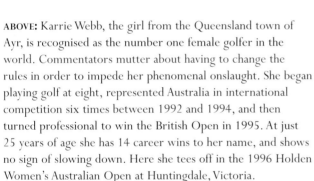

ABOVE: Karrie Webb, the girl from the Queensland town of Ayr, is recognised as the number one female golfer in the world. Commentators mutter about having to change the rules in order to impede her phenomenal onslaught. She began playing golf at eight, represented Australia in international competition six times between 1992 and 1994, and then turned professional to win the British Open in 1995. At just 25 years of age she has 14 career wins to her name, and shows no sign of slowing down. Here she tees off in the 1996 Holden Women's Australian Open at Huntingdale, Victoria.

FACING PAGE: Miss Leonora Wray (1886–1979) finds plenty of freedom for her swing as she explodes her ball from a bunker. One of Australia's golfing greats, Miss Wray won the New South Wales title four times, first in 1904. She won the Australian national title in 1907 and then again in 1908. Struck down by typhoid fever, she was forced out of the game for a decade, but incredibly returned in 1929 to win the national title for a third time. After her retirement as a player she went on to enjoy an active career as a manager, coach and general promoter of women's golf. Women have been involved in the game since its inception in Australia, staging the first national golfing championship in 1894, beating the men to it by a few months. Despite this, many golf clubs refused to give full membership to women as late as the 1980s, when the *Sex Discrimination Act* forced their hand.

ABOVE: Jane Lock was an Australian Amateur Champion and then a top professional in the 1970s and 1980s. She won three Australian championships and set course records around the world. She became known as the glamour girl of golf, attracting attention for her mini skirts and daringly short shorts. One of her most famous matches, which she won, was a head-to-head confrontation with another attractive celebrity of the circuit, Jan Stephenson, for a purse of $10,000 in the Australian Open in 1979. Fairly typically for the period, the press had a field day with the apparent incongruity of good looks and sporting skill, but the attention meant that the women's game for that year enjoyed far more spectator attention than its male counterpart.

A picture of grace in her long skirt and decorative hat is the indomitable Pearl Cole (**ABOVE**), champion rifle shot of the early 1900s, while body builder Jan Pierce (**RIGHT**) is radiating good health, strength and considerable purpose in 1986.

FACING PAGE: This photograph, which appeared in the Melbourne *Argus* in 1947, was captioned 'Here we see Violet doing the difficult masse shot'. Violet Lindrum was the sister of Walter, the greatest billiards player in the international history of the sport. Although not a professional, Violet was by all accounts a fine player, as well as being an enthusiastic advocate of the game. She set up her own billiards parlour in Sydney in the 1940s and formed an association for the several hundred women who played regularly in Sydney. She worked on improving her game by potting an average of 1000 balls a day.

ABOVE: Decorous, determined and daring are these young women of the early 1900s, who formed a football team in the name of their employer, Foy and Gibson's department store in Perth. Women's football teams are common these days, and women follow the footy as passionately as men, although the major national leagues remain very much male-only affairs.

FACING PAGE: Lawn bowls was and is one of the most popular participation sports in the country. The picture featuring a strong complement of female bowlers (**ABOVE**) was taken in Perth in the early 1900s. Today there are some 140,000 members of the Australian Women's Bowling Council, representing approximately 2200 clubs. While the sport is huge among retirees, there is a growing number of young enthusiasts as well. The players (**BELOW**) are taking part in the International Women's Bowling Carnival held in country Victoria in the early 1980s. An uproar occurred when members of the Hong Kong team came onto the green wearing shorts, a first in the official history of the sport in Australia. The precedent failed to win support among those who rule on bowling fashion.

ABOVE: In the seaside township of Torquay, Victoria, now known as the surfing capital of Australia, these trainee teachers, c.1910, have cast off their restrictive garb in exchange for modest neck-to-knees.

ABOVE: The only distance for women to swim at the Stockholm Olympics in 1912 was 100 metres, and Australians Fanny Durack and Mina Wylie, both from Sydney, came first and second, making Durack the first Australian woman to win an Olympic gold medal. And, not wishing to be impeded by a cumbersome costume that modesty demanded, she swam in a skirtless woollen swimsuit that caused the onlookers to draw breath. She belonged to the New South Wales Ladies' Amateur association, headed by the renowned Rose Scott (see page 200) who, believing that women should not compete in the presence of men, opposed the two young women competing at the 1912 games. The Swimming Association, in defiance of its own rules, upheld the wishes of the two swimmers. Between 1906 and 1921 Durack broke 11 world records. She is pictured here receiving her gold medal from King Gustav of Sweden.

ABOVE: Dawn Fraser is regarded as Australia's greatest woman swimmer: she was a gold medallist in three Olympics (Melbourne, Rome and Tokyo) and the only swimmer in history to win a gold medal for the same event in three successive games. She was at the forefront when Australian women's swimming reached new heights at the Melbourne Olympics in 1956. The 4 x 100 metres relay team of Sandra Morgan, Dawn Fraser, Lorraine Crapp and Faith Leech won gold and a world record; Fraser, Crapp and Leech finished first, second and third in the 100 metres freestyle; and Crapp and Fraser first and second in the 400 metres. But it was her personality that won the hearts of the nation – in 'our Dawn' there was something of the Aussie larrikin, a rebellious streak frequently directed at authority and convention, characteristics that saw her involved in a flag-snatching prank in the palace grounds of the Japanese emperor during the Tokyo Olympics, and led to her banishment from competition for 10 years, tragically ending her swimming career. In later life, Fraser has been a publican, businesswoman, coach and state politician. She was awarded the Order of Australia in 1998. She is pictured here (right) with Lorraine Crapp.

ABOVE: Australian women continued their dominance of world swimming in the 1970s. Born in 1956, the year Australians were cheering on Dawn Fraser at the Melbourne Olympics, Shane Gould became a teenage sensation, winning Olympic gold and breaking or equalling 11 world records by the time she was 16. Her performance at the 1972 Munich Games was extraordinary, with gold medals for the 200 and 400 metres freestyle and the 200 metres medley, and a silver and bronze respectively in the 800 metres and 100 metres freestyle. In that year she held world records in all freestyle distances. Two years later she married and retired from swimming to live in the Margaret River district of Western Australia. Recently separated, she was back as a swimming coach in 1998.

LEFT: With her sparkling eyes and bubbly personality, Susie O'Neill became the new media favourite and darling of the 1990s swimming contingent readying itself for the 2000 Olympics in Sydney. She won a bronze medal in Barcelona in 1992 followed by a gold medal (seen here) in the 200 metres butterfly in Atlanta in 1996.

ABOVE: The 'Golden Girl' of Australian athletics, Betty Cuthbert, comes to terms with her first brush with fame, as she congratulates place-getter and fellow-Australian Marlene Mathews after the 100 metres final in the 1956 Olympic Games. Cuthbert also won the 200 metres, and picked up a third gold in the sprint relay team. She captured the hearts of Australians with her shy and unassuming manner and was voted ABC Sportstar of the Year in 1956. She made a sensational return to the winner's podium in Tokyo in 1964, when she was the inaugural winner of the newly instituted 400 metres. Fellow Olympians and other Australians rallied around her in 1998 to raise money when, suffering from multiple sclerosis, she lost heavily in a bogus business scheme.

RIGHT: Marjorie Jackson grew up in the New South Wales mining town of Lithgow, and was dubbed the 'Lithgow Flash' as her athletics successes hit the headlines. She started breaking world records before the Helsinki Olympics in 1952, and dominated those games with easy wins in the 100 metres and the 200 metres. The first Australian woman to win a gold medal in athletics, Jackson retired at the age of 22 after marrying Olympic cyclist Peter Nelson. After his death in 1977, she turned her attention to charity work and sports administration. Her services to sport have been recognised by a Sportsman of the Year award (1952), an MBE (1953) and the Order of Australia.

ABOVE: All eyes are on Cathy Freeman wherever she goes. At an athletics meeting at Stawell, Victoria, in 1996, she demonstrates her marvellous free-running style. She is a champion of Aboriginal heritage and pride, and a role model for young Aborigines in sports endeavour and personal belief. She made world headlines when she carried both the Aboriginal and Australian flags after winning the 400 and 200 metres in the Commonwealth Games at Victoria, Canada. Grumpy Australian official Arthur Tunstall disapproved, but Australia applauded.

RIGHT: Lisa Ondieki shows her delight at winning a distance event at an international meeting at Olympic Park, Melbourne. Born Lisa O'Dea in Gawler, South Australia, Ondieki's long career in distance running was marked by dual marathon wins in the Commonwealth Games of 1986 and 1990, and wins in five other major marathons. Dogged by illness and injury, she has never won an Olympic title. She married Kenyan runner Yobes Ondieki in 1990.

ABOVE: Shirley Strickland in 1952 at the Australian Athletics Championships. She carried the hopes of Australia in the 1948 London Olympics and acquitted herself superbly in the 100 metres and the 80 metres hurdles, but up against the great Fanny Blankers-Koen of Holland she had to accept two thirds and a relay second. She stayed in training for Helsinki in 1952 and, as Shirley de la Hunty, was rewarded with a gold medal in the hurdles in world-record time. In 1956 she became the first woman to successfully defend an Olympic title. Strickland was a dedicated sportswoman, becoming involved with junior athletics after her retirement from competitive sport, and was awarded an MBE (1951) and the prestigious US Helms Award (1956).

LEFT: Standing only 5 feet 2 inches tall, Decima Norman (1909–83) was always referred to in press reports as 'tiny Decima Norman'. She won the Western Australian sprint title in sensational style in 1935, but was overlooked for the 1936 Olympics because Western Australia did not have a state athletics association. When finally able to compete in the 1938 Sydney Empire Games she put her age back from 29 to 21, fearing discrimination. She scooped the pool, winning a record five events – two sprints, the long jump and two relays. A press report said she ran 'like a bullet from a gun'. She moved to Sydney to train for the 1940 Olympics, which never eventuated because of the war. Back home in the west she was a state hockey player, a surf life saver, a tennis star, and a successful businesswoman and sports administrator, earning an MBE.

ABOVE: Pam Kilborn was an outstanding hurdler and long jumper. A study of style and concentration, here she bursts over the 80 metres hurdles at a club meeting in the 1960s. Kilborn came third in the 1964 Olympics in the 80 metres hurdles, and then equalled the world record for the event a few days later. She took silver in the 1968 Olympics, but her six gold medals all came at Commonwealth Games. She carried the Australian Flag at the Edinburgh Commonwealth Games, the first woman to carry a flag at an opening ceremony, and is another sporting MBE.

RIGHT: Jane Flemming has been a colourful and enduring figure in Australian women's athletics. She transformed herself from an Australian hurdling champion into a world-class heptathlete, despite many setbacks with injury. The event has seen her win medals in two Commonwealth Games – gold in 1990 and silver in 1994 – and she represented Australia in the 1992 Olympic Games in Barcelona. She won a second gold at the 1990 games in Auckland for the long jump. In an attempt to lift the profile of Australian women's athletics, Flemming resorted to rather unconventional means, modelling for magazines and a series of glamour calendars that featured beautiful athletes. In retirement she has been an accomplished sports commentator.

LEFT: One of the finest players to ever grace world tennis stadiums was Australian Margaret Smith (Court). She came from Albury but moved to Melbourne for coaching under Keith Rogers and Frank Sedgeman. Tall and strong, with an imposing presence on the court and an exemplary manner, she won a staggering 17 Grand Slam titles (for which she earned nothing in prize money because of her amateur status). Her vintage year was 1970, when she won the Grand Slam and the Wimbledon final 14–12, 11–9, in a thrilling match against Billie-Jean King. Despite her five US Open singles titles, three Wimbledon titles, eleven Australian and five French Open titles, she had to mask her nerves on the court and protect her weak second service. This photograph was taken during the Toyota Women's Classic at Kooyong, Melbourne, in 1976.

LEFT: Earlier in the century, these young Western Australian players look a force to be reckoned with and proof that the game was being played in earnest, not simply under the patronage of men as was the case in the 19th century.

FACING PAGE: The most graceful and endearing of the top players of her time, and one of the first Aborigines to succeed in international sport, Evonne Goolagong was from Barellan, New South Wales. Her talent was spotted at a young age by tennis coach Vic Edwards, and she moved to Sydney, where he coached her and became her legal guardian. In 1971, at only 19, she won the French Open and a magnificent Wimbledon final against fellow Australian Margaret Court. She made the final again in 1972, 1975 and 1976, before taking another Wimbledon crown against Chris Evert Lloyd in 1980. She married English tennis player Roger Cawley and now resides in Queensland. She is pictured here at a Melbourne suburban court in 1972.

ABOVE: The practice of side-saddle made riding a far more difficult sport for women than men. This colonial horsewoman looks in a precarious position as she takes a jump at Ensay, Victoria, c.1900.

RIGHT: Growing up in Brisbane in the 1970s, Pam O'Neill's one ambition was to become a jockey. But women were not permitted even to touch a horse on a race track, much less ride one. O'Neill led horses to the local tracks but was required to hand the reins over to a man at the entrance to the course. She campaigned vigorously against this discrimination until the rules were changed in 1979. In May of that year, she became the first woman jockey in Australia and rode three winners on her first race day. O'Neill went on to create more racing history as the first woman to win at Doomben – on Sami Boy in the Boorolong Handicap in 1979. In 1999 she was appointed chief riding instructor at the Deagon International Training Centre for Japanese jockeys.

ABOVE: A blithe spirit of Australian racing is the highly successful trainer Gai Waterhouse, the daughter of legendary trainer Tommy Smith and wife of controversial former bookmaker Robbie Waterhouse. She is known on race days for her high-fashion style, bubbly personality and irrepressible enthusiasm, but is seen here in working mode during the fervour of the spring racing carnival in October 1995. 'Of course I feel passionate about it and it shows', she confessed to *Age* journalist Caroline Overington. Waterhouse has fought hard for her place in a man's world, taking part in a Supreme Court battle for equal opportunity at the track before finally earning her licence from the Australian Jockey Club in January 1992. In just a few years she rose to the ranks of the leading trainers in New South Wales with horses such as Electronic, Stony Bay and Nothin' Leica Dane (winner of the Victoria Derby and second-placegetter in the 1995 Melbourne Cup). She holds the distinction of being the second trainer in history to win four successive Doncaster Handicaps, and was voted Australian Racing Personality of the Year for 1994–95. Respected journalist Les Carlyon said of her, 'Waterhouse succeeds not because she is a personality, but because she is a first-rate trainer'.

ABOVE: Fitness, fun, fellowship and the natural joy of running has joggers invading the parklands and pathways across Australia. The marathon became an accepted Olympic event for women in the 1980s, and in the 1990s distance running has attracted increasing numbers. Some seriously good runners were at the front of the pack for the annual Sussan 10-kilometre race in Melbourne in 1992. The winner was Krishna Stanton, number 3, with Joanna Campbell-Smith, number 9, second.

FACING PAGE: You are never too old to give it a whirl, and hammer thrower Bettina Woodburn, aged 66, does just that, at a senior athletics meeting in suburban Melbourne.

CREATIVE LIVES

Two centuries of irrepressible talent

In a rough country, where men were concerned with the business of survival, it was generally the women of 19th-century Australia who introduced the civilising influences of music, books, painting, amateur dramatics and a range of craft activities that helped gentrify humble homes. Likewise it was the women, as the chief communicators and chroniclers, who spent a portion of each week writing letters and diary entries. The struggle came when they attempted to translate amateur pleasures into professional pursuits.

The arts for women in the 20th century began to mirror the economics of supply and demand that is common to all endeavours. Women took to the stage because actresses and showgirls were needed; they wrote children's stories and women's articles because in these areas a woman's touch was thought desirable. In the areas of painting and serious literature, talented women struggled through, despite constant domestic demands. Some women, such as writer Christina Stead, avoided domesticity outright; others, such as painter Joy Hester, engaged in a precarious struggle between two worlds. Other writers, fearful of being unaccepted in a man's world, wrote under a male pseudonym, such as Henry Handel Richardson.

In contemporary times, opportunities have expanded in all areas for women, but in the arts they have positively blossomed. While this has everything to do with education and acceptance of women's talents, it is also because women, the cultural arbiters, now have economic power. They buy 80 per cent of all books sold; they fill the cinemas and organise the theatre subscriptions. They are the prime arts consumers, and what they want to see is the rendering of their experiences, be it on the page, canvas, screen or stage. This fact, combined with a surfeit of talent and a history of passionate pursuit, predicts an exceptionally healthy climate for emerging female artists.

FACING PAGE: Dame Nellie Melba (1861–1931), pictured here as Cleopatra, was born in Richmond, Melbourne, and rose to prominence as one of the greatest sopranos the world has ever seen. Like many Australians of talent she criss-crossed the globe, living the greater part of her life away from home. But Australian audiences loved her, creating record attendance figures when she returned home to sing in 1902.

ABOVE: Fanny Cochrane Smith (1834–1905) records traditional Aboriginal songs into an Edison phonograph recording machine in 1903. It was not for her musical ability that she was known, but as a cultural ambassador of sorts – one of the few people of her time, male or female, to cross the barrier between the worlds of white and black Australia. A women of 'stature, intelligence and charm', she married a white man, but maintained strong ties with her community in Oyster Bay, Tasmania. She was a successful businesswoman and community leader, and possibly the last full-blood Tasmanian Aborigine to survive, a fact recognised by the Tasmanian Parliament in 1884.

RIGHT: Irish-born singer Lola Montez came to Australia in 1855, stayed just two years and was the sort of woman respectable parents feared their daughters might become, should they be allowed onto the stage. She was said to have been the lover of Liszt and Mad King Ludwig of Bavaria. She was beautiful, loud, excitable and smoked cigars in public. Lola's erotic 'spider dance' aroused Melburnians to a state of fascinated frenzy. She played at Ballarat at the height of the gold rush, where her famed fight with the editor of the *Ballarat Times* concluded with the two attacking one another with whips. Another local paper reported it as a 'combat [that] raged with more than Trojan Fury'.

FACING PAGE: Respectable women did not pursue stage careers until well into the 20th century, but amateur pursuits were encouraged, particularly those of a musical nature. Here an aspiring drawing-room violinist, Mary MacIntyre, practises in the backyard of Fairseat (home of Queensland Surveyor-General, Walter Hume) in Bardon, Brisbane, in 1897.

LEFT: Dorothea Mackeller (1885–1968) was 19 when she penned one of Australia's most well-known poems, *My Country,* which contains the oft-quoted lines: 'I love a sunburnt country / A land of sweeping plains…' She went on to write three volumes of poetry and three novels, but her subsequent work never had the impact of her popular signature poem. She has been described as typical of women artists of the period in that her surfeit of inspired, youthful energy eventually dissipated through lack of use. This photograph, showing a bareheaded and barefooted teenager, was taken at about the time she wrote *My Country.* The poem was inspired by the sight of a long drought breaking across the northern New South Wales landscape, where her wealthy Sydney family owned property.

FACING PAGE (BELOW): Dame Mary Gilmore was born in 1865 near Goulburn, New South Wales, to a farming family. She trained and worked as a teacher before becoming involved in a radical utopian movement in the 1890s, which marked the start of a lifetime commitment to social causes ranging from Aboriginal welfare to feminism and socialism. From 1910 to 1954 she published eight volumes of verse, with many poems advocating her passionately held ideals. Paradoxically, she is best known for the extraordinary portrait of her by artist William Dobell in 1957 rather than for her own prolific output and tireless campaigning for social good. She received the rare (for a writer) honour of a state funeral in 1962.

ABOVE (LEFT): Henry Handel Richardson (1870–1946), born Ethel Florence Lindsay, became Australia's greatest late 19th and early 20th-century novelist. She left Australia as a young woman and lived most of her life in Europe; but drew consistently on the country of her birth for the themes and settings of her stories. Of her novel *The Fortunes of Richard Mahoney* (1917), in which she used the Australian landscape as a metaphor for one man's decline, she said, 'I dropped a European book into a struggling literature'. Her influence on future generations of Australian writers was immense. Her best-known work (later a film), *The Getting of Wisdom* (1910), was based on her time spent as a student at Presbyterian Ladies College, Melbourne. Like many women of her time she was an avid diarist, as well as a musician of considerable talent.

ABOVE (RIGHT): Ethel Turner (1870–1958) migrated to Australia at the age of nine. She worked mostly in the genre of children's literature, a mould she tried to break out of, but was discouraged by her publishers from doing so. Her best-known work, *Seven Little Australians*, written when she was just 24, was probably the first book to deal extensively with the experience of Australian suburban childhood. The death of the heroine in the story is one of the most moving scenes in Australian literature. A wife and a mother of two, Turner often referred – indirectly – to the competing demands of the creative and domestic spheres.

No one could match Dame Nellie Melba until the rise to stardom of Joan Sutherland in the 1950s. Born in 1926, Sutherland abandoned a career as a secretary when she came to public notice via a local singing competition. Her stunning success in *Lucia di Lammermoor* at Convent Garden in 1959 (**LEFT**) set her on the path of the opera greats. Her nickname, La Stupenda, is an indication of the breathless wonder with which she was regarded. She retired in 1990, but emerged in 1992 to greet the Queen (**ABOVE**), who personally awarded her the Order of Merit. Dame Joan took the opportunity to lodge a complaint about Australia's Republican Movement. 'I'd like to put them all on Fort Denison', she said, referring to the old convict prison island in the middle of Sydney Harbour.

FACING PAGE: Olivia Newton John (left) and Pat Carroll at Essendon Airport, Melbourne. The two performers paired up with considerable success in the 1960s, and again in the 1980s in a Los Angeles retail venture, Koala Blue. Olivia went on to a successful solo and film career, notably the musical smash-hit *Grease*. She has proved to be one of the great survivors of the precarious entertainment industry, and of life itself. She turned her brush with breast cancer into a crusade for recognition and better research funding for the disease.

FACING PAGE (ABOVE): Backstage of *Nice Goings On*, Sydney, 1935. Photographer Sam Hood captured on film the girls from what was commonly known as the Pony Ballet backstage at the Theatre Royal. The girls had to make a number of quick changes throughout the evening, keeping hair and make-up intact, all in very cramped conditions.

FACING PAGE (BELOW): From the 1930s to the 1950s, the Tivoli theatres in Sydney and Melbourne were part of what was known as the Tivoli Circuit. Productions were at first very much in the old revue tradition, incorporating fantastic scenery and costumes and long lines of singing and dancing chorus girls. This group was known as the Tivoli Ballet. The two other types of performers were the soubrettes, who were usually selected from the ballet for solo spots, and the 'nudes', topless performers who were carefully arranged on stage for artistic effect. In accordance with obscenity laws, the nudes were not allowed to move at all on stage.

ABOVE: Circus Oz was founded in 1978 as a radical departure from traditional circus performance, and is still going strong both in Australia and overseas. The group has maintained a passionate interest in breaking down gender expectations in terms of what performers can achieve physically, and one of the delights of watching the shows has been the display of strength and vitality on the part of the female cast. Photographer Ponch Hawkes took this underwater shot at the State Swimming Centre.

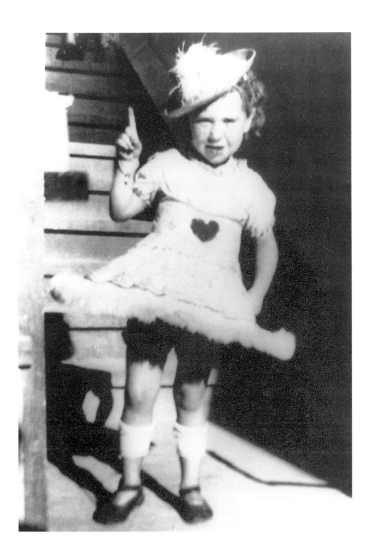

LEFT: Young Australians of the 1940s, 1950s and 1960s grew up with a number of variety stars who moved around the country, becoming as familiar to their audiences as the family next door. Jill Perryman is captured here in her debut in *White Horse Inn* in 1936, a budding entertainer at the ripe old age of three. She went on to have a very successful stage and television career, including starring roles in such 1990s hit musicals as *The Boy from Oz*.

LEFT: Toni Lamond is pictured here with her son Tony Sheldon. The extended family included the likes of Stella Lamond and Helen Reddy. Lamond remembers how she and her husband, Frank Sheldon, travelled with a young child: 'Most of the time we lived in hotels, with Tony in the bottom drawer'.

ABOVE: Kate Ceberano is one of Australia's most dynamic and sensual performers, crossing musical barriers wherever she finds them. Born in Melbourne in 1966, she has had a string of hit singles and albums and has won a long list of music awards throughout the 1980s and 1990s. In 1992 she gave a stunning performance as Mary Magdalene in the concert version of *Jesus Christ Superstar*. In her professional life, she relies on the support of a close-knit circle of family and friends.

ABOVE: The film *Picnic at Hanging Rock* (1975) was based on the novel by Joan Lindsay, which tells the story of the disappearance of schoolgirls from a St Valentine's Day picnic in 1900. The evocative story, which set young innocent girls against a backdrop of mysterious bushland and ancient geology, was an instant hit, tapping into the ambivalence that white Australia has always had about the landscape. The film revived interest in Joan Lindsay as a novelist, reintroduced the idea of women's films in Australian cinema and launched director Peter Weir's international career.

FACING PAGE: Classical ballet is still one of the most popular extracurricular activities for young girls in Australia, some of whom stick at it and eventually go on to become members of the Australian Ballet, which is regarded as one of the best ballet companies in the world.

ABOVE: This photograph, *Sunday Reed with Joy Hester Carrying Sweeney* (1945), was taken by Hester's then husband, artist Albert Tucker. Hester was the only female member of the radical art group, the Angry Penguins, which emerged in the 1940s as a response to the conservatism of the day, and is one of Australia's most individual and posthumously successful artists. Sunday Reed was a wealthy patron of the arts, who sponsored Hester and oversaw the creation of her magnificent property at Heide, now Melbourne's Museum of Contemporary Art.

LEFT: The National Gallery School of Victoria, 1900. There is a surprisingly large number of women among this group. While girls were encouraged to paint for recreation, and attendance at art school was tolerated, full-blown careers as artists were very rare for women until the 1940s and 1950s.

FACING PAGE: Emily Kame Kngwarreye was born in about 1910 in country to the north-east of Alice Springs as a member of the Eastern Ammtyerre language group. She began painting late in life and in the eight years before she died in 1996 produced around 3000 works of art. They were of such quality that they established her as part of the international art scene. Her output has been described as 'so prolific that it will be some time before the results of this remarkable energy are fully understood'.

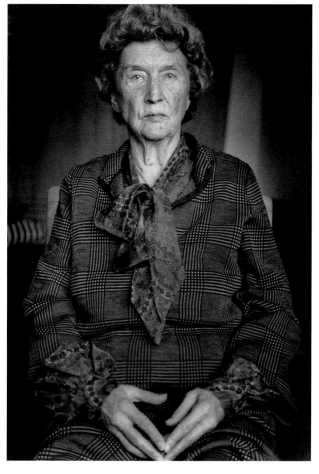

ABOVE: Internationally acclaimed Australian film star Judy Davis made her debut in the leading role of *My Brilliant Career* in 1979, a film based on the book by Miles Franklin. Stella Maria Sara Miles Franklin (1879–1954) was born in Talbingo, New South Wales, and wrote *My Brilliant Career* as a teenager. She drew on her own experiences to tell the story of Sybilla, a hot-tempered character who rejects love in order to pursue her career as a writer, a radical concept for the time.

RIGHT: Christina Stead (1902–83), born in a harbourside suburb of Sydney, trained as a teacher and worked in an office before leaving Australia to spend most of her life abroad. She wrote her first novel in the 1920s and was published in the 1930s. Her most famous novel, *The Man Who Loved Children* (1940), is set in Baltimore but draws on the character of her tyrannical father. A writer of considerable psychological insight, she said that 'personality [was her] private passion'. She is widely acclaimed for her verbal brilliance and literary experimentation.

FACING PAGE: Judith Wright is one of the greats of Australian poetry. She was born in northern New South Wales in 1915, later returning to the family's country property and starting to write poetry because the 'country seemed to me very beautiful and very threatened'. She has remained an avid environmentalist, a concern reflected in her work, which also deals eloquently with Australian culture and the more intimate aspects of relationships.

ABOVE: Sally Morgan, photographed at the Adelaide Writers Festival in 1992, is one of contemporary Australia's most compelling storytellers. Her book *My Place* (1987) was a publishing phenomenon, drawing on the themes of place, memory and belonging. She has written a number of other books and a successful play, *Sister Girl*. Morgan is also an accomplished artist and her work has been exhibited in the United States, United Kingdom, India, Japan and Germany. She is currently head of the Centre for Indigenous Art and History at the University of Western Australia.

FACING PAGE: Helen Garner has been one of the leading lights of Australian literature. Born in 1942, Garner was a teacher before being sacked for talking about sex in class. She turned to journalism and then wrote one of the most influential novels of the 1970s, *Monkey Grip*, a tale of drugs, love, dependence and rejection. In 1995 she turned her hand to non-fiction in *The First Stone*, an account of a sexual harassment saga played out at the University of Melbourne's Ormond College. The book generated one of the most passionate debates in the history of Australian feminism.

ABOVE: *The Moth of Moonbi* was made by Charles Chauvel in 1926 and dealt with the corruption and redemption of a young bush maid, played by Doris Ashwin, who goes to the city, finds it full of greed and returns to the moral cleanliness of the bush and a jackaroo who loves her. The film deals with the tension between the city and the bush at a time when there was a massive shift in population to the cities; it was not unusual for a female character to be used to embody these kinds of social dilemmas.

RIGHT: Annette Kellerman was a swimmer turned entertainer and film star, who was voted 'The World's Most Perfect Woman' in an American poll taken in the early 1900s. She shocked Bostonians when she wore this revealing swimsuit, with some reports claiming she was arrested. She pre-empted celebrity workout videos by several decades in garnering a mass audience for her often eccentric beauty routines. In one of her films, *Daughter of the Gods* (1916), she was required to dive 28 metres into the sea, setting a world diving record for women.

ABOVE: Gillian Armstrong is Australia's most notable female film director. Born in Melbourne in 1950, she went through film school in the early 1970s. Her break came when she directed *My Brilliant Career*, which was the first film to be directed by a woman in Australia since the 1930s; it went on to win her six Australian Film Institute awards including Best Director. Her local films include *Oscar and Lucinda* (1997) and *The Last Days of Chez Nous* (1991), while in her overseas career she is best known for her adaptation of *Little Women* (1995).

ABOVE: June Jago appeared as Olive in the original 1955 production of the groundbreaking Australian play *Summer of the Seventeenth Doll*. The play was not only remarkable for its realistically portrayed Australian themes, but also for how tenderly and intelligently it dealt with issues particular to women's lives. This last factor helped make the female roles long-lasting favourites among Australia's female actors.

LEFT: Ruth Cracknell bears the mantle of the Grande Dame of Australian theatre. Her professional career started in the mid-1940s in radio. Since then she has appeared at most theatres around the country in a staggering diversity of roles. Her film credits include *The Chant of Jimmy Blacksmith* and *Emerald City*. She has an imposing presence and carries big dramatic roles with ease, but she is also one of the country's finest comic actors, a fact proven by her rendition of a mother living with an adult son in the award-winning television series *Mother and Son*.

ABOVE: Rachel Griffiths did not pass her auditions with any of Australia's major acting schools, which is probably why her talent is still so delightfully all her own. She came to attention in the Australian suburban classic *Muriel's Wedding*, in which she played the hard-bitten but tender-hearted friend, and made an enormous impact for her role as the sister in the British film about Jacqueline de Pre, *Hilary and Jackie*, for which she was nominated for an Academy Award as best supporting actor. She is seen here in a 1998 Melbourne Theatre Company production of Henrik Ibsen's *A Doll's House*.

RIGHT: Robyn Nevin's career is one of the most successful and prolific careers in the 'industry'. She began in the 1960s after training at NIDA. As an actor she has moved easily between the mediums of stage, film and television, playing most of the classic roles and picking up a swag of awards on the way. As a director her trajectory has been equally spectacular. She has worked with most of the major Australian companies on a variety of plays; she has promoted new and interesting work; she spent several years as artistic director of the Brisbane Theatre Company; and in 1999 she was appointed to the top job in Australian theatre, artistic director of the Sydney Theatre Company.

ABOVE: Melbourne-born Kylie Minogue began performing as a child, but came to prominence in 1987 as the star of the television soap *Neighbours*, which is probably Australia's most successful television show ever, claiming 45 million viewers around the world at the height of its popularity. On leaving her role as Charlene, the nation's favourite teenager, she went on to become an overnight sensation as a pop star, recording smash hits such as 'I Should Be So Lucky' and 'Locomotion'. She has successfully revamped her image several times, once by working with Australia's prince of darkness, rock star Nick Cave. She is an undisputed celebrity both here and abroad.

FACING PAGE: Ruby Hunter is a traditional-born Aboriginal woman from the Ngarrindjeri Kukatha Pitjantjatjara tribe of South Australia. When she was eight she was taken from her family and raised in white foster homes. She began as a singer after a period of hard times and raising children. With partner Archie Roach, she took to the road, busking and performing at festivals and small venues. Their most famous song, 'They Took the Children Away', based on their common experience of forced removal from their families, was to play a significant role in publicising a shameful chapter in Australia's history.

ACKNOWLEDGEMENTS

The authors would like to thank the following individuals for their generosity in providing images for use in this book: Melanie Beddie, Diane James, Linda Kavanagh, Peggy Kavanagh, Jacinta Le Plastrier, Libby Lester, Bridget Ohlsson, Geraldine Ohlsson, Heather Pearson, Pamela Skelton-Cox and Jane Woollard. Particular thanks to Libby Lester for her invaluable editorial assistance and help in the compilation of material, Peter Ascot for his patience and care in laying out the pages and his keen editorial eye, the media staff at the Australian Bureau of Statistics, Melbourne, and the City of Yarra Library network. Special thanks to Faruk and Stella Avdi and Bruce Postle for their support and tolerance during the long hours of work. Finally, grateful acknowledgement is made to the many public and private organisations who have provided photographs and information including: The Age: 192, 201, 209 (left), 232, 234 (below), 268; ALLSPORT: 233 (below); Archives Office of Tasmania: 25, 68; Australian Broadcasting Corporation: 113; Australian War Memorial: 99 (044516), 148 (H11576), 154 (A03962), 155 (top H11567 & below P01908.007), 157 (J0360), 158 (136390), 160 (43964), 161 (087663), 162 (top 000304/1 & below 136831), 164 (112827), 166 (GIL/67/0483/VN), 167 (below P1735.010), 193 (119674); Battye Library (WA): 20 (10090P), 24 (28014P), 70 (9815P), 106 (WA Historical Society 24400P), 110 (Mr Neil Mitchell 29429P), 222 (top 9831P), 228 (26876P), 229 (top 9579P), 238 (below 5523P); Cobar Regional Museum: 90; Conservation Commission of the Northern Territory: 93 (Bradshaw); David Moore: 146, 187; Department of Infrastructure, Victoria: 171 (below); Edith Cowan University, Museum of Childhood Collection (WA): 35; Fryer Library, University of Queensland: 125 (top), 246; Ponch Hawkes: 55 (1976), 57 (from Kensington Oral History Project 1992), 86 (from 'Relatively Speaking – The Family in words and pictures' 1995), 87, 92 (below/part of the ACTU's Art and Working Life project 1988), 119 (from the Women and Work Kit 1979), 172 (below), 253 (from Circus Oz show 'Aqua Profunda' 1977); Herald & Weekly Times: 44, 46 (below), 63 (top), 234 (top), 236 (top); Italian Historical Society/CO.AS.IT.: 54 (top), 62 (below), 72 (top), 73 (below right), 105 (below), 170; Jill White and Associates: 22, 40, 138; John Oxley Library: 50 (top), 96, 134; David Johns: 175; John Lamb: 8, 76, 85 (below left), 97, 111, 133, 137, 172 (top), 173, 174, 194 (top), 214; Lauraine Diggins Fine Art: 258 (top); Mary MacKillop Centre, courtesy Trustees of the Sisters of St Joseph: 205 (below); The Mercury: 184; Melbourne Theatre Company: 266 (top), 267 (top/Jeff Busby); Jennifer Mitchell: 38, 39 (below), 45 (top); Jacqueline Mitelman: 205 (top), 209 (right), 216 (top), 255, 260, 261 (below), 263, 265, 267 (below), 269; Mortlock Library of South Australiana, State Library of Australia: 126 (B26830), 202 (B10324), 204 (B10324), 217 (B53550); Museum of Chinese Australian History:

19 (below), 58 (below), 73 (below left), 128, 168; Museum of Victoria: 17, 43, 53, 56, 81 (below), 104, 124, 132 (top); 222 (below), 230, 240 (top); National Archives of Australia: 12 (top A1200, L39802), 125 (below A1200, L70664), 189 (below A1200, L69338), 190 (A6180/6, 10/4/75/62), 249 (top left A1200, L3693); National Film and Sound Archive: 257 (courtesy Peter Weir), 261 (top/courtesy Margaret Fink Films), 264 (top/courtesy Curtis Brown); National Gallery of Australia, Canberra: 13 (Axel Poignant, Aboriginal girl and new born baby, 1942, gelatin silver photograph, 32.8 x 28.4cm), 22 (Olive Cotton, Australia born 1911, Party frock, 1938, gelatin silver photograph, 35.5 x 29.9cm), 58 (top/James Pinkerton Campbell, Australia 1865–1934, Filling the boiler, 1905, gelatin silver photograph, 20.4 x 13.4cm), 60 (From a bound album of 210 albumen silver photographs, 1868–70, 29.5 x 26.4cm), 112 (Pat Stuart, Lady Louis Mountbatten's press conference, Canberra, 1946, gelatin silver photograph, gift of Mrs Pat Stuart, 1982), 145 (below/Olive Cotton, Australia born 1911, Fashion shot, Cronulla Sandhills, 1937, gelatin silver photograph, 30.4 x 38.5cm [image] 40.2 x 48.7cm [sheet]); National Gallery of Victoria, Melbourne: 51 (Edna Walling [1897–1972], gelatin silver photograph, 20.2 x 25.3cm, presented by Mrs Barbara Banes, 1983); National Library of Australia: 12 (below), 14, 15, 16, 31 (top), 48, 52, 59, 80, 82, 83, 92 (top), 103, 115 (below), 127, 139, 142 (below), 169 (top), 171 (top), 181, 211, 216 (below), 227, 233

(top), 236 (below), 244, 249 (top right), 252 (below); National Trust of Victoria: 42 (top); Leah Olver: 176; Pan Macmillan Australia/Peter Johnson: 194 (below); Noel Pascoe: 240 (below); Performing Arts Museum, Victorian Arts Centre: 250 (below), 251, 254; Powerhouse Museum (Tyrell Collection): 28, 151; Bruce Postle: 27 (below), 36 (below), 37, 39 (top), 74 (top), 77, 85 (top & below right), 96 (below), 98, 102 (top), 105 (top), 109, 113 (top), 114 (below), 117, 118, 135, 141, 143, 145 (top), 183 (top), 188, 189 (top), 190, 196, 203, 206, 207, 215 (top left), 218 (top), 219, 220, 223, 225, 229 (below), 235, 237, 238 (top), 239, 241, 242, 243, 250 (top), 256, 262, 266 (below); Random House: 120 (below); Fiona Robertson-Cuninghame: 218 (below); Royal Historical Society of Victoria: 180; Royal Women's Hospital: 11; State Library of New South Wales: Govt Printing Office Collection 26, 30, 95, Holtermann Collection 10, 153, Hood Collection front cover, 18 (top), 27 (top), 29, 32, 100, 102 (below), 130, 140, 147, 156, 163, 185, 210 (top), 252 (top), Mitchell Library Collection 21, 248; State Library of Victoria: 49 (top), 50 (below), 62 (top), 66, 71 (top), 88, 152, 226, 247 (below), 249 (below), 258 (below); Office of Senator Natasha Stott Despoja/AUSPIC: 215 (top right); Tasmanian Museum and Art Gallery: 247 (top); University of Melbourne Archives: 73 (top), 91; Senator Amanda Vanstone: 215 (below); West Australian Newspapers: 195; Greg Weight: 259.

SELECT BIBLIOGRAPHY

Australian Dictionary of Biography. Vols 1–14. MUP, Carlton, 1966–1996.

Australia's Yesterdays. A look at our recent past. Readers Digest, Sydney, 1974.

Book of Australian Facts. Readers Digest, Sydney, 1992.

Bremer, Stuart. *Living in the City.* Dreamweaver, Sydney, 1983.

Burke, Janine. *Dear Sun.* Heinemann, Melbourne, 1995.

Cannon, Michael. *A History in Photographs.* Currey O'Neil, Melbourne, 1983.

Cannon, Michael. *Australia in the Victorian Age: 3: Life in the Cities.* Thomas Nelson, Melbourne, 1975.

Cannon, Michael. *Australia: The Spirit of a Nation.* Currey O'Neil, Melbourne, 1985.

Clark, Manning. *History of Australia.* Abridged by Michael Cathcart. MUP, Carlton, 1993.

Country Life in Old Australia. Currey O'Neil, Melbourne, 1982.

Davies, Alan. *Sydney Exposures.* State Library of NSW, Sydney, 1991.

De Vries, Susanna. *Strength of Spirit.* Millennium, Sydney, 1995.

Dixson, Miriam. *The Real Matilda.* Penguin, Melbourne, 1994.

Dunstan, Keith. *The Amber Nectar.* Viking O'Neil, Melbourne, 1987.

Elder, Bruce (ed.). *The A to Z of Who is Who in Australia's History.* Child & Associates, Sydney, 1987.

Epstein, Anna (ed.). *The Australian Family.* Scribe Publications, Melbourne, 1998.

Fixed in Time. Fairfax Library, Sydney, 1985.

Grimshaw, Patricia et al. *Creating a Nation.* McPhee Gribble, Melbourne, 1994.

Hall, B. & Mather, J. *Australian Women Photographers 1840–1960.* Greenhouse, Melbourne, 1986.

Hall, Rodney & Moore, David. *Australia: Image of a Nation 1850-1950.* Collins, Sydney, 1983.

Horne, Donald. *The Story of the Australian People.* Readers Digest, Sydney, 1985.

Issacs, Jennifer. *Pioneer Women of the Bush and Outback.* Lansdowne, Sydney, 1990.

Jones, Shar. *J. W. Lindt: Master Photographer.* Currey O'Neil, Melbourne, 1985.

Kingston, Beverly. My Wife, *My Daughter and Poor Mary Ann.* Thomas Nelson, Melbourne, 1975.

Larkins, John & Howard, Bruce. *The Young Australians.* Rigby, Sydney, 1981.

Luck, Peter. *A Time to Remember.* Heinemann, Melbourne, 1988.

Luck, Peter. *This Fabulous Century.* Lansdowne, Sydney, 1980.

McConville, Chris. *Mum and Dad Made History.* Museum of Victoria, Melbourne, 1988.

O'Keefe, Daniel. *Australian Album.* Daniel O'Keefe, Sydney, 1982.

Postle, Bruce. *Capturing the Moment.* Heinemann, Melbourne, 1995.

Reilly, Dianne & Carew, Jennifer. *Sun Pictures of Victoria: the Fauchery–Daintree Collection 1858.* Currey O'Neil, Melbourne, 1983.

Ritchie, John. *Australia as Once We Were.* Heinemann, Melbourne, 1975.

Ross, J., Hutchinson, G. & Geddes, M. *Australia's Olympic Century.* Ironbark, Sydney, 1998.

Russell, R. & Chubb, P. *One Destiny!* Penguin, Melbourne, 1998.

Spender, Dale. *Writing a New World.* Pandora Press, Sydney, 1988.

Stone, D. & Mackinnon, S. *Life on the Australian Goldfields.* Methuen, Sydney, 1976.

Thompson, Elaine. *Fair Enough.* University of New South Wales Press, Sydney, 1994.

Usher, R., Postle, B. & Lamb, J. *Images of Our Time.* Viking O'Neil, Melbourne, 1989.

Vanderwal, R. (ed.). *The Aboriginal Photographs of Baldwin Spencer.* Currey O'Neil, Melbourne, 1987.

Who's Who in Australia 1999. Information Australia, Melbourne, 1998.